KATZEN

KATZEN

(CATS)

Christopher Abiodun Stephen

authorHOUSE®

AuthorHouse™ UK
1663 Liberty Drive
Bloomington, IN 47403 USA
www.authorhouse.co.uk
Phone: 0800.197.4150

Scripture quotations marked KJV are from the Holy Bible, King James Version
(Authorized Version). First published in 1611. Quoted from the KJV Classic
Reference Bible, Copyright © 1983 by The <u>Zondervan</u> Corporation.

Published by AuthorHouse 07/03/2015

ISBN: 978-1-4969-9565-0 (sc)
ISBN: 978-1-4969-9564-3 (hc)
ISBN: 978-1-4969-9566-7 (e)

Print information available on the last page.

Any people depicted in stock imagery provided by Thinkstock are models,
and such images are being used for illustrative purposes only.
Certain stock imagery © Thinkstock.

This book is printed on acid-free paper.

CONTENTS

INTRODUCTION

Katzen 4:10-13....Katzen is a Deutsch word for cats, it sounds interesting but this book is not an agricultural book and the title makes it look like one, the code in the front of the word is meaningless to those who have not seen or read the other copies of my three books. Cats are animals that are known for having a great basic instinct, the sense of feeling, for these particular animals, is very high, they can perceive odour of things from a far distance, also they can see, therefore people are said to be cats if their behaviours resemble those of these, particular group of animals. The cats can see and keep quiet but the dogs will see and bark.

The quality of seeing and keeping quiet made most people to like the cats more than the dogs, most people in this category are the spies, investigators, informers or men of the underworld, but while some of them are like the cats, the others are like the dogs because they cannot keep quiet. The question then arise, and it is that, why are some people monitoring the other ones?, is it for good or for evil?. Are they looking for information?, are the cats looking for technological secrets? Or are the national cats trying to safeguard their territories from invaders? Why are cameras on the streets, in offices, in sensitive commercial areas where there are banks, courts and police stations? In internet, why do we have spywares or software for spying, why is one company monitoring the progress of another company in terms of annual profits, and staff quality? Do the people want to buy shares and invest their wealth or money? Do they want the best companies for investments, in order to make more money? These are the little reasons why some innocent people turn into cats in order to monitor the affair of others. Some people really monitor the other people and companies, in order to invest and make great profit, nothing more but others and nations does so for security reasons. For security purpose, people and nations also monitor other nations.

In nature, everything is dual and opposite, good and evil, man and woman and so on. The answer for, why some people may be monitoring the other, may be both, for evil and for good, before I answer this question fully, first I want to analyse why I think that people go into hidden or secret places.

Behaving like cats is dated back to a long time ago when the people for the fear of unknown, think in their minds that their lives or existence are threatened or insecure, and they separate themselves from the crowd, meet and decide what happens in the societies, the reason for meeting separately may be economic, social, political, geographical and or religious, it depends on every individual. The secret meetings provided the answers to the problems of these set of people, as decisions are made in their favor and I think that, this is how the secret societies came into existence. Since the formation of most of these secret societies, smart cats have become many in existence, while some are individual; others are in the organisations working for one group or the other.

While some people like to behave like the cat for economic reasons others have political motives, those that have social and geographical motives are not many.

Majority of the people who wants power at all cost turn into cats because they have political motives, and they watch the activities of their opponents in order to plan ahead, some people knows the plan of their opponents and they move to destroy those plans before they actually mature, purely out of hatred and envy or just for power show. Most people in this group also monitor the financial capability of their opponents and if it is good, they destroy them so that their opponents don't have enough money to go ahead with their political plans. Some of the readers of this book may ask, why this is so, if the motive of these opponents is correct and to save the people? I think that the few powerful cats with great economic manpower at the top, always feel disturbed, if they see other people trying to rise up, and because they want to remain very few and stay at the top, they sort of stay invisible and cause problems for the others who want to rise up to the top like them. Another question then arise again, it is the question of whether someone can rise up to join them at the top?. The answer is YES and I think, it is possible with a condition. Those that are their children but with other names, can rise up without any condition and stay at the top with them, but those that are not their children, if they join the correct secret societies, then they can stay with the few at the top also. The situation is easy for the children of these few cats because they were born into the secret societies and they rose up easily with their parents. For security sake, I think the condition is to join the correct SECRET SOCIETIES.

Whichever reason, we may be having for becoming cats, as I said before depended on every individual. Therefore cats in this book ONLY refers to the smart and very sensitive people who work in secret, in order to achieve their aims and safeguard themselves, a nation or an institution.

The major reasons for cat's actions, apart from economic and political ones could also be that-

a. Each cat is trying to deliver his people from bondage.
b. The cat is trying to correct what is wrong in the society and protect the nation that he belongs to, against external invasion and intruders.
c. They just want to dominate their fellow countrymen.
d. They want high positions, recognition, money and fame.
e. Some cats go into actions when their existence is threatened.

There are different types of cats, and their motives are also different. We have organisational, national, individual, intelligent, societal and the local cats.

In short, the major purpose of most cat actions is to bring peace to reign in their communities and nations. Happiness and cordial relationship among the people also make the cats to act sometimes.

In the natural cats, the behavioural problems, such as avoiding the litterbox, excessive meowing and other attention-seeking behaviour, biting and painful or destructive scratching are also found in the humans and can be corrected by first eliminating physical causes, then instituting a program of gradual retraining. Remember that there are no bad cats, or bad humans but only uninformed cat caregivers or trainers. It means that, if a trainer refused to handle his cats well, there will be poor results; the cats will not perform to the best standard expected.

It is proper to deal with one problem of cat behaviour at a time. Too many "dos" and "don'ts" will only confuse the cats and frustrate the training attempts. It is better to start with the most potentially hazardous problems first such as chewing on electrical cords and then move on from there. The same thing happen in the human circle, whereby the human cats are trained to do special jobs at a time, the toughest problems or trainings are always giving at first, to make the trainees adapt fast and the other less tough exercises come later, to be learnt.

Cats' aggression toward people can be caused by poor training as a kitten (as shown in play aggression), fear, or other factors. Teaching how to prevent a cat's aggression toward people, and how to deal with it when it happens, and how to curb a cat's biting and scratching behaviour always happen during the training session. During the training of special human cats, fear and unnecessary aggression are removed from the mind of the trainees and after graduating from the training school, all the trainees are posted to their various working zones to implement what they have learnt so far, to the benefit of their employers. Most human cats also have trainers and the lives of these people are in their hands, because the trainers control and manipulate them.

While there are different types of humans, White, blacks, or brown living in different regions of the world, so there are different types of cats and one of them is Abyssinian Cat.

The Abyssinian is described as lively, curious and tireless, and with patience and affection, it will bond to its human companion for life. Lithe and lovely with its glorious colour and ticked coat, this cat is a real winner in popularity.

We can learn more about the delightful "Aby" through these "http://cats.about.com/pets/cats/library/breeds/snapshots/blaby.htm" _Abyssinian Cat Breed Snapshot_

The quickest way to find pertinent information about the Abyssinian cat, and its suitability as a pet.

Although there are a number of theories about its origin, the history of the "Aby" is mired in the ages. That it is one of the oldest known breeds of cat that lends credence to the assumption that it may have been an early offshoot of the African wildcat, ancestor of all domestic cats. The photos demonstrate that heritage.

We also have the big cats namely the Lions, Tigers, and the Leopards. They have the same behavioural pattern of life like the small cats. They are carnivores, smart and sharp; they dominate other animals in the jungle.

Natural cats in the wild or jungle also watch and monitor the lives of mates and that of the less wild ones, just as the humans. The top cats, the lions, tigers and the leopards know the secret behaviour of the other animals, and this make them to be able to dominate in the wild successfully.

Majorly, the reason for writing this book is to show, that there is order in the universe and that things don't just happen for happening sake, because some human cats make them to happen. And there is a saying that, every environment shows the type of people living inside it, if it is well organised and clean, it means that the human cats there, are knowledge-able and have the technical know-how for living good, they know what to do at the right time, no much protests or complaints from the people and this made them to conquer their environment. But if it is the other way round, it shows that those in such a place are still yet to know, everywhere is dirty, and the people complain and protest all the time for one thing or the other.

The world is full of delusion, illusion and confusion but only the wise cats can live adequately fine in it, I mean, the cats that really belong to the secret order of arrangements. Protesting on the streets does not solve any problem as I feel because those who are in the intelligence or in the secret orders have their rights given to them without complaints and those that do not belong are not part of the society and they are goats. This means that going to the street on protest means, going there to die. Probably, this is the reason why Jesus said that many people have eyes, ears but cannot see and hear what happens in the kingdoms of the world. The kingdoms of the world are the kingdoms of God and God created the world in seven days.

There are also many paths in this world, namely the path to survival and the one to destruction, the path to good and the one to evil, the path to happiness and the one to sadness, it is like everything is dual in nature. While some human cats are causing good things to happen, others cause or make disasters to occur, all in order to confuse peoples mind, so that individuals would not find the way. The human cats are as dangerous as the real big cats in our forests.

I entered my own PATH at 27 with a clear vision of willing to survive and I started spiritually with the temples and the spiritual schools because I learned that it is better to seek first the kingdoms and that every other thing would be given later to the true seeker. On my path, I found four different schools of thought and this made my heart to make tick tack sound with my eyes and mind wide open. The first school of life is traditional and full of illiterates and children, someone can enter into this school through family members or through friends or alone and virtually every kind of human cats can be found here. The percentage of the learned cats is very low and women with children can also be found in this place. In this school, people believe whatever they are told without asking any question because most information are passed across to members by the elderly and most traditional people whom we believe can never tell lies.

Immediately, my mind told me that I don't belong here and I continue to search for another school of life where I can find many learned and enlightened ones. I found an English school of life and my mind told me that I belong to this one, I felt so happy despite the fact that most people of the world condemns the first school and this new one, that I have just found. I felt so happy because of the logical wisdom that is being passed across to me by this new school which the outsiders cannot partake of.

The smaller and mushroom churches preach and confuse peoples mind against this my school but I never get worried because of what I am learning from it. It was when I got to the higher stage of this school that I know that majority of the cats confusing the minds of the people against the schools are themselves part of these schools, meaning that they are wolves in sheep`s skin.

Then my mind told me that they were not doing well because they want the people to die in ignorance and secondly, they don't want them to see the light. It was at that time too that I know that light can be found where some cats called darkness.

I continued on my path and I am happy thinking that there are no other schools. Many people till today feel this way and they stopped searching for the other ways, grow old, some happy before they die, while others died unhappy. Some had their missions fulfilled while others had theirs not completed, some cats even failed to continue to learn. And in fact, why are there many schools of life? The answer is clear, and it is just to bring confusion and delusion into people`s mind because the confusing question in the minds of the people will be, which one is correct and up-to-date?.

My path was and it is still full of all sorts of cats, some really know what they wanted, others are confusionists, many listened to what the small cats were saying and they left the school, discouraged, they had no vision. I kept going on, on the path though it was tough, not talking to the people and keeping what I know to myself because no one would understand me. Any time, I try to tell the people, in a form of advice; they just would not believe me. I went to the University, passed out, worked briefly, and in my land, sometimes there is work, and sometimes too there is none but I am happy most of the time and not disillusioned. With my academic knowledge and the little one that I gained from my school of life, I moved to Europe, hoping to make the money and feel on top of the world, I connected with the branch of my school of life in England, Europe and I continue to learn more wisdom hoping that life would be more easy for me but the reverse was the case. In Spain, I could not find work, then I became confused and I started thinking of what could be the problem, after going through some vocational courses that can give me some jobs- I am academic and I felt that my school of life, supposed to help me but it didn`t. The human cats here, are very wicked, they know that I receive my monographs, study them and after go out to look for what to do to survive, especially work but I could not get any, as at this moment my thought was that, a brother should help another brother but I was wrong. Occasionally, I go to the temple, tell my white colleagues to see whether they can lead me to what I can do but no help came to me. I suffered a lot in Spain.

There are too many human cats on my path, the rich and the poor ones, impersonating and disturbing my survival plans, some, with the same name, same date of birth etc. I could not understand why this was so and questions like are there other schools of life higher and better? or what is happening? or am I competing with other people?, comes to my mind often or probably life is a competition but I am not seeing any competitor?. These questions made me to alter my data or dates, so that other human-cats will never find my true position in life, it worked for me but I never knew what the magic was. Then I found my second church and two scriptural books were given to me--the book of Mormons and the pearls of great price, in the first book, a statement supported the bible by stating that, in difficult times of our lives, there are things that the lord want us to see which we are failing to know, and so we must be searching our minds and the scriptures always. I thought I have got everything I needed for survival in life-enough school education and spiritual one, but I still continue to search--is there another school of life, here in Spain different from the English one? I found another one of the same nature- no difference, they are saying the same thing and both the Spanish and the English people know that I am a pupil in these schools but why is my social conditions not changing for the better- still no work and no comfort. I decided to move away to another land with the mind that there are still other hidden mountains undiscovered.

Now I have grown to full adulthood and I have not got what I want. My path is not an easy one and I became very unhappy like most other people but undaunted or unconfused, I encountered so many human cats here in Spain and also I learned so many things from them. Life is interesting, most of them would say to me, and I know that to be true already.

I left to Germany and here is better for me than Spain. It was in Spain that I lost most of my time but nonetheless, I learned the most basic way to search better and that is, with computer, Spanish people teach to the cats, free of charge in most of their academic schools, some of the basic useful computer programming that is good for survival and the keys/ the uses, given to every student, this is my only gain from Spain.

Here in Germany, I found many schools including the golden one which makes this place different from Spain and my eyes were fully opened when I got here. There are many sensible human cats in this place and life is comfortable, here telling lies on someone do not work because the leaders know many things before they happen, discrimination is everywhere but here in Germany it is minimal and it is like they know who you are even before you enter this country. My explanations are necessary because there some people that are today passing through similar situations and my advice is that they should never lose hope.

For someone who understands and is watchful, the lessons or the digests that are being sent to the pupils of the golden school carry information that leads someone to the other schools, where the real GOLD can be found. Unless a watchful human cat understands the lessons being passed across, he or she would think that he has got the real path that leads to the gold and would not search further.

Nobody who finds gold wishes to tell the other person. And even if one wishes to tell the other person, such other person will never believe, I tried it, by telling my white friends that I feel there is still another school but they told me that there is no other one and they never believed me, I was surprised.

I think that they never believed because both of them were so comfortable- they were having everything that can make someone to be on top of the world, they can buy whatever, or go wherever and if you say that there is gold somewhere to somebody, the first question will be- what type of gold is it? Because many Germans are even living fine and most of them, don't even travel to see other places. Even the poorest Germans are comfortable and from their allowances, given to them by the government, they can eat and go to places. This is wonderful.

The human cats, especially the leaders, in this place are clever, they made the people comfortable, to the extent that, no one would like to go and commit crime, money machines are left in the open and no one cares to steal from them. When someone is okay, why should he commit crime?-- this is why I think that making the people comfortable is a special tool for combating crime. The poorest German can buy and maintain a car, if he wants because a second hand car costs between seven hundred and fifty euro to nine hundred euro but they don't even want because with fifty euro in a month, transportation is easy. This situation is also possible in the other European countries.

I was lucky to see from my lessons, that there are still other schools, I checked and it was true. I went to the schools and found that they exist. I sat in their lodges, filled my forms and submitted. I am happy. The cats all over the world could not believe their eyes and while some of them are happy with me, the crazy and jealous ones are very sad. Only an intelligent person can get the riddles leading to the gold, solved and I am happy I discovered the answer through my school digest which told me that only a silver plated art work is covering the door leading to the final golden world- which to me means that, the final golden school is still out there and not this present one, I searched for it immediately and I got the answer---Eureka!!! I found it.

Now I know that, all along I have been wasting my time, the knowledge of the computer is good. The golden schools are in all the countries of the world, that I passed through before coming to this place but they are so hidden that only the prudent eyes can find them. In NIGERIA, my country also, there are lot of them but I am grateful to the Germans for this golden school that has saved me. I have entered through the first two doors in Germany, I sat in the lodges, I feel the comfort but now, I need to go home and enter through another door of the same school, then I am totally free. The readers of this book should believe me that gold can only be found through a Golden school.

Some cats found the gold through their parents who are members of the existing lodges. Also there are many lodges but only few are REAL and golden.

Good friends on top of the mountains saw me, but they could not call me to sit with them in the golden lodges. They want me to come inside by myself, this confirms my saying that nobody would ever find the way to gold and show it to his friend.

I wish that the readers of this book would find the way that I have found, through sweat and hard work, without having to leave their various countries. So mote it be. Gold is where we are but only that we need special skills to actually find it.

And I want to appeal to the lords of every land, to support whoever has found the way to these golden lodges, there are many lodges and temples in every land but the golden ones are different and unique because only the WISE and PRUDENT ones can find them.

Everyone has his own path but this is my own

The school-ROF- with few educated ones and the rest illiterates- I never attended, my own first school-red rose. 2, second school-blue rose. 3, the third school with two mountains a, the golden schools b, golden lodges

All these schools have double faces-red/ blue groups- dualism-no explanation

1, smallest mountain 2,bigger one 3, another bigger one 4, the biggest mountain-the eye.

BUT ALL ARE HIDDEN FROM OUR EYES- no one will tell you that they exist.

Some human cats passed by me, to the top and I am happy they did, some of them promised that, I will never be alone with my problems or that my problems would never conquer me, but really, do I have a problem on my path? Definitely, it is only one and it is, that there are many cats that are traitors, disturbing my work activities.

Now I can hear, see, feel, smell and taste better, meaning that my five senses are at alert and well developed through these spiritual schools, that I have passed through. I thank all those that passed me by and are still loyal to me. They are lords, when I am in difficulties and I cry out, some of them that are good to me always hear my voice and come to my rescue. My own knows me and I know my own, also I am very happy that the greatest and the most powerful set of human cats, are on my side.

This is not to say that everything is perfect with all the human beings and myself, because we should not forget that we are in a crazy world of delusion but no matter how crazy the world is, the anointed ones would make it.

Human cats would see everything that is going on, no matter the situation and my final action is that my 45th lord succeeds in getting to the top of the mountain and when this happens, my mission is completed and my prediction written in my second book has come to pass, so shall it be. The first four got to the top without anyone knowing or suspecting but only I and very few other people, know.

41,B 42,B 43,B 44,B and 45,B

All along on my path, these eminent cats have saved me, by one way or the other and I am grateful to them. I hope that when the 45th cat gets to the top like the others (in 2016), his getting there would not spell doom for my life and for the lives of Bill and his boys/girls), so help me lords.

They are red and blue. They are also the eye in the middle of my two palms (left and right) and we have been together secretly for a long time.

I entered my real spiritual PATH at 27, left the University at 29 and up till now, that I am 52, I have still not got to the top of my mountain. I like to start to move to the top of my own mountain, through the senate or through the governorship route like the other brothers on the path.

Would I ever get to the top of my own mountain? Only a ninja can block a ninja which means that only °ME° can block °ME°. I know the way to the top and I have successfully put myself to guide °myself° there. Who are °myself°? °myself° are the B`s, 41,42,43,44,45. And in my land- OS and IBB. Therefore if I fail, °myself° have blocked °me° but I feel that I will not fail. It does not matter when I get there but I like to get there. So help me lords.

Does the bible support these intelligent activities?

YES, 1 Corinthians 4 verse 5 said - The secret purposes and motives appear in the unerring register, for God will bring to light the hidden things of darkness and will make manifest the counsels of the hearts.

Isaiah 65 verse 6 to 7 said that- Behold, it is written before me, I will not keep silent, but recompense, even recompense into their bosom. Your iniquities and the iniquities of your fathers together said the lord.

Also Mark 13 verse 35,36, and 37 talked about watching and praying all the time, so that we don't fall into temptation. To me, this verse shows that the devilish cats are at work while the anointed of the lord are also at work but if we are not careful we can fall into the hands of the devilish cats and our individual life would not be as we want it to be.

Life existence is for us to live it and learn of both the good and the evil in the world. God has done well by trying to let us see that HE is God and that there is order in the universe. He made the good and the evil and he guides us through to see, achieve and give praises to HIM. I am not so religious but I think that God had done the right thing, by putting the kingdom of the good and the kingdom of the devil and he commanded us to seek his kingdoms first- the two, and understand perfectly what is going on, then whatever we are looking for, in this life would be giving to us. Those who move ahead working, building and giving birth without seeking the kingdom first are not heeding or giving ears to the warnings of the lord and they sometimes march on problems that lead them to their destruction. The lord wants us to be smart like the natural cats, by saying to us, in Mark and Matthew that many have eyes and ears but cannot see or hear what is happening in the kingdoms, HE also said in John 8:32 that if we seek to know, we shall know the truth and the truth shall make us free from our iniquities.

Always the bible is talking of the REGISTER which means that the lords have all the records of all the activities gathered through intelligence by the smart cats, whether the cats are negative or neutral or positive. Let us all imagine a situation whereby things are not alright, for instance roads are bad, no water to drink or for bathing, no dresses, no information gadgets like television sets or radios, no enough houses to live, no records, no cars, and even no work. How would our lives be?. Definitely we will curse God and wonder why we are here on earth. But thanks be to the lords that He made all things to be available and He controls the cats to work accordingly, through His records, so that everyone would experience peace and happiness.

The lords are the cats and they are ordained by the Almighty God to work according to his principles in order that universal peace might be experienced by the anointed ones. The plan of salvation, must also be followed because, it is ordained of God and the lord uses everyone including the human-cats to make the plans to come into fruition. The activities of the cats must also be towards guiding the sacred truths that will lead towards building a virile and standard world, by this I mean that the truthful situation of things would be revealed to us all, and the people would be aware, in order to know and behave properly. No one will wake up and starts to look for what to do as everything had been arranged down for the people to get, for instance whatever anyone wants is there, name it, schools, food items, cars, work and houses and the environments are well organised too.

Organisational cats can be found in the various organised businesses that you can name. Some are employed by these organisations so that they can work for them; others are planted there to monitor what goes on, inside the same organisations. Some of these workers are visible while the other ones are invisible, those that are invisible may be on the payroll of the same organisations or on the payroll of another company which may also be invisible. But the truth is, he who pays the piper must dictate the tunes, this situation makes life very complex and no one knows exactly the motives of the next person sitting next to the other. It is just like the biblical parable of the sower where the real farmer has sown his crops and the negative cats in the night, sowing the weeds among the good crops, without the real farmer detecting immediately. In this case, the farmer detect the weeds after both the weeds and the crops have grown up together, this is a real life situation and it has been so, from time immemorial, nothing can change it, therefore the bible and the Quran said that we should watch and pray always. The good cats work so that the goal of the organisations, that they work for is reached while the bad cats, sometimes prevent the real goal to be reached and the organisation folds up, it depends on the force at work, if the positive force is greater, then the organisation survives but if the negative one is greater, the organisation falls. In the organisations, the leaders too should not witch-hunt the cats, working for the good of the organisation because un-necessary disturbance of the people sometimes make life difficult, making workers not to put their best to work.

Some cats in the organisation, work and learn and later grow-up as better citizens, forming their own firms and becoming rich while others see and never learn, this is the real life situation, they never want to learn because they allowed their minds to be carried away by the things of the world. Some cats learn very fast but they are slow in the implementation of their plans, probably because there is no capital and there is no help, these set of cats if they cannot find good partners to work together with, often fail in their bid to become good citizens, setting up their companies and bringing up the economy of their country.

Normally, a business must be started with a little capital and from this little capital, more money is made. Therefore it is always better to start to work on something that is profitable.

The federal or national cats are almost the same as the organisational cats but the little difference is that the cats in the federal service are paid by the nation or the federation. The nation dictates what she wants and the cats follows the rules, those that refuse to follow the rules are kicked out of service, therefore the nations most of the time achieve their goals undisturbed but when all the cats here cooperate negatively to defraud the nation, then the nation involved run at a loss, meaning that the gross domestic product of such nation is low or in the red. When this type of situation occur, the good cats see and like to come in, to rectify the situation in order to make the people to enjoy their lives, by putting into places the correct social amenities and life continues. These cats operate in the vineyard of the lord and the wise ones would learn and after form their own businesses and become better persons. Each federation in the world helps its citizens through trainings up to the University level, sometimes through vocational studies or on the job learning, so that the people too can contribute to the activities of the government in return. The people makes the nation and if they are of good quality through various trainings, the standard of such nation too, improves but if the percentage of illiterates in a nation is high, then such nation too, will not grow economically and politically.

Individual cats, either work privately or work with the federal service or with the big organisations. The cats under this category are mostly specialised professionals like accountants, lawyers, military personnel, teachers and so on.

As I said earlier, anybody can be a cat, no matter the profession of the person involved. Most of these professionals use powerful electronic gadgets like computers, machines, telephones and with the necessary software, to achieve their aims. The cats here may be negative, neutral or positive, just like the ones, in the other establishments and they might have worked in the federal service or in other big organisation before becoming individual workers in order to achieve greatness or good living. Those who cannot form their own companies continue to work with the existing firms until they achieve what they want. It is correct that the individuals who refused to see or hear, would not achieve success.

And lastly, the geographical and religious cats, are found in most geographical regions of the world and in the religious circles, and they watch over the work of the lords too. In those days or even up till now, the kings make use of the cats under this category, to watch over their domains and subjects, what the subjects talk or the type of opinions or protests that they give in the public, are all known by the kings even when the kings are not there physically, the cats inform them of what goes on in the kingdom. Religious cats also watch over the churches or the mosques, and the social life goes on undisturbed.

In the society, the activities of the cats often lead to the arrest of criminals by the police. In short, the people that are cats within each nation, does more good than evil but the few ones who like to do evil often find themselves in jails. Sometimes the cats misinform the kings or the rulers probably to score a point or to cause confusion but wise kings or rulers are always ahead of time and things that happen, in the society and they know and adjust accordingly.

The wise kings or rulers often designate geographical zones with different types of cats, the positive thinking ones in a zone, and the negative ones in another zone, also the neutral ones in a separate zone but all report to him, the activities of each zone. As the king or the ruler, he knows the cats and rewards them accordingly.

The religious cats know all the activities of the house of worship and they make sure that all the activities goes on peacefully without problems, the problems of the worshippers are also solved and the people are happy. The religious cats also act as guides to the new members, by giving answers to their questions, they help to distribute the holy books like the bibles, teach and sometimes baptise the members in the church, they see and know the new ones in the congregation, they also see and know the bad guys who has come to disturb the service and they send them out. Later all the work done in the house of worship may be reported to the leader who invariably may report to the king of the land, in short, the religious cats perform well and allow harmony to reign supreme in the worship place and in the region where the house of worship is located but sometimes too, they may be negative but they are instruments of the lord and his work on the surface of the earth. Each house of worship has a mode of worship and special garments. and after the day`s worship, everyone moves home in their normal dresses. Each geographical zone contributes harmoniously to the state that it belongs to, the state contributes harmoniously to the nation and the topmost man or woman with the other people in the society are happy.

CHAPTER ONE

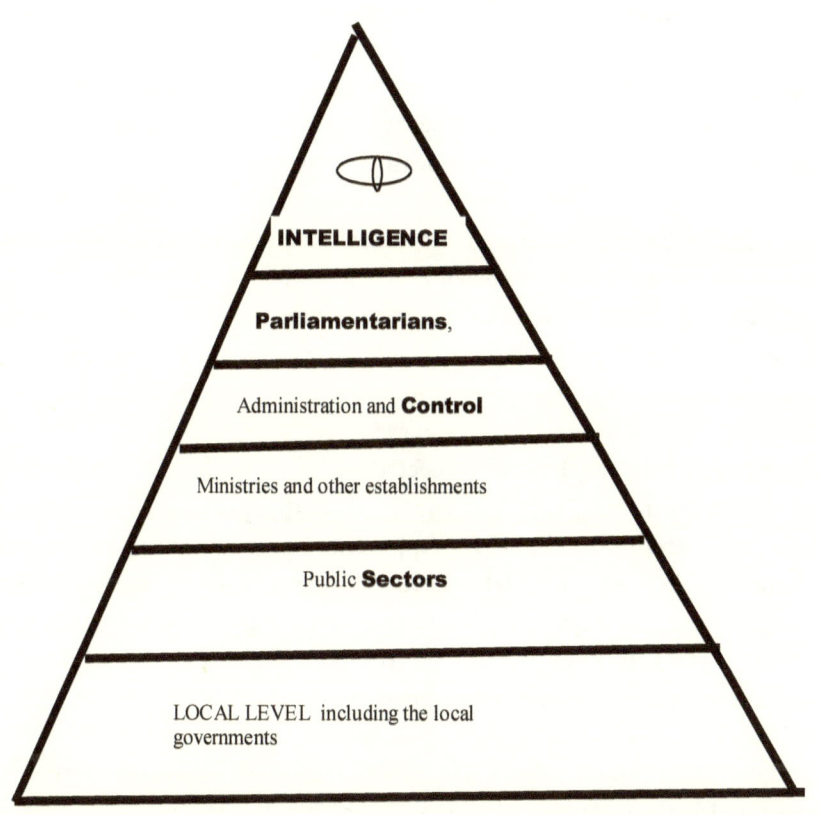

INTELLIGENCE WITH OTHER CADRES OR LEVELS

In my own opinion, espionage can lead to cold wars and normally cold wars can never end. When we think that a cold war has ended, a new one starts or replace it, I think this is because `new walls` are being created everyday and it is these walls that brings into existence these cold wars. And what do I mean by walls? To me, due to conspiracy, actions are put into places by cats and they watch how the people react to these actions. The cats being used are the walls that prevent other countries from achieving their aims and this type of situation makes various countries to spy on one another, in order to know where the problems are and to solve them.

Traditional espionage has changed, with new threats coming from non-traditional countries, the ending of most cold wars, in my opinion, does not reduce the amount of espionage because each day of the year brings new economic, social or problematic situations or threats from nations, which can invariably affects other nations of the world, therefore cats or joint forces must also increase in number, to assess the situation and make peace to reign. The issue of world peace is very vital to the survival of most nations of the world, both economically and politically.

The search for more power and the ability to dominate completely make nations to spy on each other, also for security purposes. Most big cats make sure that neighboring countries are not making programs that will bring chaos or problems to the region. Borders or frontiers are watched with cameras and also guided by armed forces.

The citizens help the FBI to protect the U.S. from foreign intelligence aggression by raising security awareness and reporting any suspected espionage activity to the FBI. Apparent espionage activities include attempting to view or steal records or plans without authorisation; eavesdropping on conversations through phone bugging; asking questions without a need, to know certain information; keeping unusual hours; or working outside the normal office areas.

In the United States, the FBI protects the civil rights of people by investigating the violations of federal civil rights statutes and by supporting the investigations of state and local authorities in certain cases. This act is performed through the cats and through the Federal civil rights violations that fall into several categories: hate crimes motivated by bias against such characteristics as race, religion, national origin, and sexual orientation; color of law crimes involving law enforcement and related criminal justice professionals' misuse of their right to discretion, such as use of excessive force or police misconduct; involuntary servitude or slavery.

The most typical civil rights violations occur only when there are riots and civil disobedience and the common complaint involves allegations of excessive use of force by law enforcement personnel causing injuries or death. Another common complaint involves racial violence, such as physical assaults, homicides, verbal or written threats, or desecration of property.

When these violations occur, many citizens that are not rich enough to seek for justice, sometimes riot or protest to let the world know what is happening, they also put their representatives forward to talk to the authorised people that can render help to their problems but those that are rich always can seek for justice and be compensated.

The FBI collects and keeps information statistics on serious crimes reported to law enforcement agencies. The categories are murder, forcible rape, robbery, aggravated assault, burglary, larceny-theft, motor vehicle theft, and arson.

Keeping records is very good because it makes the country to be guided correctly and safely. It also allows the justice department to monitor the rate at which crimes are being committed and the percentages of criminals comparable throughout the year and in the years ahead.

On drug trafficking, the FBI has determined that the most effective means of combating this crime is to use the enterprise theory of investigation, which focuses investigations and prosecutions on the entire criminal enterprises rather than on individuals.

The effective means of combating drug trafficking truly is to stop the criminal enterprises from selling to the buyer and when the buyer does not have to buy then the society is free of drugs but in most cases the cats arrest the buyers on the streets and in their houses and leave the criminal enterprises. The task under this category for the cats is a very hard one, and this is the reason why total combat of drug crime is still impossible till this day, no one is sure of who is actually behind the criminal enterprises and so I think, it is a delicate job for the cats.

When asked: How can we stop people like you? Popeye responds:
"People like me can't be stopped. It's a war. They lose men, and we lose men. They lose their scruples, and we never had any.. I don't know what you have to do. Maybe sell cocaine in pharmacies. I've been in prison for

20 years, but you will never win this war when there is so much money to me made. Never."

Really someone like Popeye can never be stopped because there are many invisible cats under him and many of them are even in the security departments of most nations of the world and they are richer than even the presidents. This trade can never be stopped and the traders themselves don't care if they die because at short times, a lot of money is made.

I refer to these people as VICIOUS cats that do not care of what may happen to them or to any other person as long as their billions are coming in. They are vigilant and well equipped for the drug work

A cat that is not strong enough can offend the big guy on top and get himself killed. Drug trafficking started long time ago and it is still going on but I think, it has not stopped probably because it is an easy way to be rich. Most very rich cats are in this category and unless you are a cat yourself, you can never know them because they are into big businesses to cover up.

The Central Intelligence Agency (CIA) is an independent US Government agency responsible for providing national security intelligence to senior US policymakers. This organisation has a lot of cats like the FBI

When Mikhail Gorbachev came to power in the 80's he made sweeping reforms in the KGB. As a result the KGB became less aggressive towards political dissidents and curtailed its struggle against foreign countries.

In august 1991, KGB Chairman Vladimir Kryuchkov led a failed coup against the government. It was the beginning of the end for KGB. This event and revelations about other activities, including the infiltration of Russian Orthodox Church, created popular demand for the reformation of KGB.

Russian president Boris Yeltsin split the organization after Soviet breakup. As a result, five agencies were formed, each with a separate function. KGB officially ceased to exist on 6th November, 1991. Today's KGB or the Russian new secret service under Vladmir Putin has witnessed great changes and it functions well just like the American intelligence. Most nations including Russia also have exchange security programs that serve all. The cats under the Putin administration are very effective, and this may probably be the reason why there is peace in the whole of Russia. The old USSR got split up, under President Boris Yeltsin, and autonomous states were formed and put into place before President Yeltsin left the government. But the total reign of peace in this area, came to be, when President Putin steps into government, as there were grumblings, rivalry and politics among the citizens of the autonomous states before he stepped in. The cats under Putin were able to move in and resolve most of the problems, elections into the parliaments, senate and into the leadership of these autonomous states were conducted and won. I think the excellent performance of President Putin was due to the fact that, he is a cat and a long time member of the KGB.

Russia makes a lot of money from the sales of firearms, ammunitions and other military equipments, to other countries of the world who may need them to solve their national and international problems, for instance, protecting and safeguarding their borders from external aggression. I think that this country also buys the weapon-models, it is not manufacturing, from other nation like the United States of America.

Italy under Silvio Berlusconi and under the previous leaders also had a powerful intelligent service. Under Berlusconi, we heard more of the Sicily Mafia groups coordinating and working together with the Italian Mafia groups but nevertheless the government was able to put up good programs which raised the Italian economy greatly before Silvio left power. The Italian intelligence is similar to those of other nations and also it is well connected.

Germany
Bundes Nachrichten Dienst (BND).

BND has 8 different branches operating in their own jurisdictions. These divisions include...
Technical Support (Technische Unterstützung)
Security & Defense (Sicherheit)
Analysis (Auswertung)
BND School (Schule des BND)

Administration (Steuerung und zentrale Dienstleistung)
Signals Intelligence (Technische Aufklärung)
Organized Crime and International Terrorism (Organisierte
Kriminalität & Internationaler Terrorismus)
Human Intelligence (Operative Aufklärung)
BND performs its operation in the foreign countries only. The agency
is similar to American CIA in this regard because it cannot conduct
domestic espionage.
The Office for Protection of the Constitution "Verfassungsschutz" is
responsible for the local intelligence services.
The German military has its own intelligence agency known as Military
Screening Service or "Militärischer Abschirmdienst".

In 1920, German socialist movement started. This movement was initiated
by 'The Nazi Party', also known as the 'National Socialist German Worker's
Party'. As a result of this movement the 'Third Reich' (third German
empire) was established.

The empire was led by Adolf Hitler, who was Nazi leader from 1933 to
1945. The Nazi government established an intelligence agency known as the
'Nazi Intelligence Network'. Later it was named as Gehlen Organization.
But nowadays, I noticed that most of the intelligence activities of Germany
follow also the pattern of the American intelligence.

The intelligence reports regularly to the Senate Select Committee on
Intelligence and the House Permanent Select Committee on Intelligence.
The Intelligence Oversight Act and various Executive Orders dictated
this structure. Under this present regime of Chancellor Angela Merkel,
the intelligence work perfectly and there is always peace within the cities
of Germany. The problematic situations of those days are forever gone,
foreigners or visitors come and go away without problems, workers every
morning go to work, business people go about their businesses and everyone
lives without fear of intimidation or loss of life. Renovations and building
of new roads are done, gardens for relaxation and recreational activities are
made for the enjoyment of the people and also new coaches or wagons of
fast trains were bought and installed, in fact most places look new. Before
Chancellor Merkel, was Chancellor Gerald Schroder, he governed well
also, by making the German economy the best during his time, machines

and robots were put to do most of the dangerous works very fast, in the motor assembly plants of BMV, Mercedes and in the oven assembly units of Bakeries where the workers cannot work under high temperatures, the human beings does the less dangerous parts of most jobs and work goes on, fast and quickly too.

I was not inside Germany, when Chancellor Schroder got elected but I know vividly that he contested with Chancellor Helmut Kohl, who was the leader of the Eastern Germany then, while he was the leader in the Western part of Germany. Before the Berlin wall fell Kohl was in the eastern part that runs a communist government and according to the news, life in the eastern part was terrible to the extent that people were jumping over the fence into the western part of Germany. This situation made the United Nations, Amnesty international and very many other eminent personalities to come together to help the eastern people by making sure that the wall is removed. I watched most of the ugly situations on television and videos and I was so grateful to Chancellor Kohl that, without problems he accepted that the Berlin walls should go and they went. I am so grateful to God also that the twenty fifth anniversary of the incident met me right here in Berlin, where I saw the pictures of the walls at various locations and white balloons used to mark the places where the walls stood as at that time. The most fascinating thing that I notice now is that chancellor Kohl after all those rigorous years could still be looking young and good. The intelligence in the eastern part of Germany, I know, would not be very different from the one in China and the old Soviet Union. Today, I think the Germans are having a mixed intelligence just like my country Nigeria, that is running a mixed economy. Now we have the CDU, the SDP and the other smaller parties in this country, they form coalition, run the nation and all the people are happy. The top cats in Germany are coordinated by these great people and here you can find powerful robots, machines for industrial works, also machines for wars.

The German intelligence is smart, good, and things are done always according to the law and there is no discrimination. The social, economic and political sectors of the country contribute adequately to the success and progress of the German nation during the time of Schroder. Presently Merkel also is contributing more to what chancellor Schroder had done.

The information can be seen in the financial times and in the Stock exchange manuals.

Germany military strength under the government of Chancellor Merkel also witnessed a great increase because of new and modern equipments which were acquired. New personnel were recruited also, to make sure that the situation is good. The defence statistics, are as follows;-

PERSONNEL

Total Population: 81,471,834 [2011]
Available Manpower: 36,417,842 [2011]
Fit for Service: 29,538,413 [2011]
Of Military Age: 790,368 [2011]
Active Military: 148,996 [2011]
Active Reserve: 355,000 [2011]

LAND ARMY

Total Land Weapons: 4,539
Tanks: 408 [2011]
APCs / IFVs: 1,794 [2011]
Towed Artillery: 1,500 [2011]
SPGs: 185 [2011]
MLRSs: 252 [2011]
Mortars: 200 [2011]
AT Weapons: 200 [2011]
AA Weapons: 400 [2011]
Logistical Vehicles: 10,400

AIR POWER

Total Aircraft: 783 [2011]
Helicopters: 433 [2011]
Serviceable Airports: 549 [2011]

RESOURCES

Oil Production: 156,800 bbl/Day [2011]
Oil Consumption: 2,437,000 bbl/Day [2011]
Proven Reserves: 276,000,000 bbl/Day [2011]

Partial Sources: US Library of Congress; Central Intelligence Agency; Fighting Forces (Barron's)

LOGISTICAL

Labor Force: 43,350,000 [2011]
Roadway Coverage: 644,480 km
Railway Coverage: 41,981 km

FINANCIAL (USD)

Defense Budget: $41,000,000,000 [2011]
Reserves of Foreign Exchange & Gold: $180,800,000,000 [2011]
Purchasing Power: $2,940,000,000,000 [2011]

GEOGRAPHIC

Waterways: 7,467 km
Coastline: 2,389 km
Square Land Area: 357,022 km
Shared Border: 3,790 km

NAVAL POWER

Total Navy Ships: 90
Merchant Marine Strength: 421 [2011]
Major Ports & Terminals: 9
Aircraft Carriers: 0 [2011]
Destroyers: 0 [2011]
Submarines: 4 [2011]
Frigates: 15 [2011]
Patrol Craft: 0 [2011]

Mine Warfare Craft: 20 [2011]
Amphibious Assault Craft: 2 [2011]

Equipments and Support

To achieve victory, simply having the best personnel and paraphernalia is not enough. It is essential that people and equipment are delivered to the right place at the right time. Commentaries here offer insights into the tools being used to provide commanders with the right capabilities when they require them. The Germans are very good in equipments maintenance and most of their cars, aircrafts, trains and buses are always new as old cars are not allowed to ply the roads. The roads are clean and neat at all times and the cars and the buses ply the roads without any problems, the traffic lights work perfectly also and there is no delay. They have the best and the strongest military equipments in the world, they also have secret bunkers located in strategic cities.

There are support companies that changes old equipments into new ones all the time and staff are trained on new and up-to-date programs. The internet has support with Microsoft Company because Microsoft updates software and makes them available to the industries. The German intelligence cats are smart and they make the people to be smart also, through info boards in the train stations or airports or bus stations, the people are informed of everything, arrival and departure time, other information concerning the nation is sent to the screen for the people to know without seeing the cats sending them.

There is a cultural event among the German cats, and this event comes up every October, it is called the Octoberfest. During this time, the cats from various countries gather together to celebrate and exchange pleasantries, it is a special time whereby all the cats dress up in different cultural attires. Some of the people paint their faces like the real cats and others just dress normally. Car owners park their cars and walk around, it is a special time when there is no showing of pride, and the rich cats mix together to eat and drink with the other people of the world. During this time also, someone can easily see the mayors and the governors of various states among the people, also eating and drinking, this notable example, gives to me the assurance that all the foods and the drinks are safe for consumption and the foreigners are happy to see this example by themselves.

Israel
Israeli Mossad

Mossad history starts almost immediately after the inception of the State of Israel.

In 1949 'Central Institute for Coordination' was set up to improve coordination between the Shabak, AMAN and political department of the Foreign Office. It was under the control of Foreign Ministry.

In 1951, CIC was replaced by Mossad under direct supervision of the Prime Minister. In June 1951 Mossad signed a clandestine agreement with the American CIA.

Mossad has a diverse range of operational activity and the operational methods for defending Israeli and Jewish interest are extremely crude in the olden days.

The agency has been known to kidnap torture and kill individuals, manipulate journalists and politicians and monitor various organizations and individuals but today, we are witnessing a new dimension, and there is no more torture and killing like before, and I think that, this may be due to the efforts of the joint task working together for a long time to bring peace to Israel and the Middle-east.

Mossad is one of the most effective intelligence organizations in the world. It operates in many important countries, including the Middle East.

The largest number of Mossad agents work in the United States where they collaborate with American intelligence agencies and are known to influence American Middle East policy. The same thing happens in Israel, where the Americans intelligence also monitors the activities of the Middle East and reports back to the Americans and the rest of the world. Under the present regime of president Netanyanhu, I can see that the regime's intelligence coexist with the American intelligence, in order to bring a lasting peace to the problems of the middle east, other countries intelligence are also present as observers and they report back to their people. Ehud Barak, who was also an ex-president of Israel and now the defence minister under Netanyanhu, assists excellently, the government of Netanyanhu, to bring a lasting peace to Israel and the Middle-east. Just as Ehud Barak did, Ariel Sharon also did his best for Israel, before he fell into coma and taken to the hospital but now, he is very well and he lives peacefully in his home. In the middle east zone where there are problems at all times, we can find a lot of cats here, trying to watch, hear and report back to their employers, for example, the journalists and the media reporters. Life in this area is sometimes terrible, military cats firing missiles and the negative ones also firing back, cats-reporters taking pictures and reporting the incidents to the appropriate quarters, all in the name of world peace but today it is a bit peaceful if compared to the last twenty years, when the problems of crossing borders into Israel by Palestinians, were common. Rocket and gun firing is at a minimal level as at today and I think that praises should be giving to the entire world intelligence communities.

The problems of Israel and the Palestine people can be traced back to many centuries and part of the stories can also be found in the bible, whereby these two groups of people are always having problems with each other. The bible had it, that the Palestinians are unbelievers while the Israelites are the children of God. This is true, but the modern day countries which constitute the old Palestine nation, now have children of God, who are Christians and the old idol worshipping mode of life, is no longer common with the people, moreover most of the native Palestinians had migrated to other lands as a result of too many conflicts in the zone and today many of them are Christians in other lands. There are churches, in these area and we can see the people converting from their old religions into Christianity but the problem is that the leadership of the countries which constitute this old Palestine, is still Islamic, i.e, the leaders are Muslims while other people still belong to some other religions. When problem comes, all the people are said to be unbelievers because of the leadership and they are killed. The true cats know the truths, sometimes the leaders are Muslims in the physical but in actions, they are Christians or that they belong to Hinduism or Buddhism. And why is this so? I think that the reason is that it is very difficult, to change the old religious tradition, nations that had been noted to be Islamic from time immemorial with a lot of fanatics cannot change to another religion all of a sudden because the people will not follow. Any attempt to change the national religion may lead to chaos and the leaders assasinated. This is why a cat must find out the real truth, so that the real truth will make him or her free, sometimes religion brings a lot of complexities or complex situations.

Another issue that causes problem between Israel and the neighbouring countries is the issue of nuclear armament, each country intelligence watches out for danger always, and this is good for safety purpose. All nations having nuclear armaments must know the capacity of their counterparts having nuclear weapons, and also the leaders must be friendly to each other otherwise a nation, with a crazy leadership can one day rise against the other ones. The United nations security council is very good in the monitoring of member nations, so that problems that could lead to wars does not happen and this is done through various meetings, checking and decision making in the parliament.

Member nation that does not comply with UN decision is fined or other appropriate punishment given. The human cats in the UN are the most important, in the world because of this monitoring activity that is being carried out every time, there is need for it.

Military strength of Israel, under the government of President Netanyanhu has witnessed a great increase because of the new and modern equipments which were acquired. New personnel were recruited also, to make sure that the situation is good. The defence statistics, are as follows;-

PERSONNEL

Total Population: 7,473,052 [2011]
Available Manpower: 3,511,190 [2011]
Fit for Service: 2,963,642 [2011]
Of Military Age: 121,722 [2011]
Active Military: 187,000 [2011]
Active Reserve: 565,000 [2011]

LAND ARMY

Total Land Weapons: 12,552
Tanks: 3,230 [2011]
APCs / IFVs: 6,278 [2011]
Towed Artillery: 550 [2011]
SPGs: 706 [2011]
MLRSs: 138 [2011]
Mortars: 750 [2011]
AT Weapons: 900 [2011]
AA Weapons: 200 [2011]
Logistical Vehicles: 7,684

AIR POWER

Total Aircraft: 1,964 [2011]
Helicopters: 689 [2011]
Serviceable Airports: 48 [2011]
yOil Production: 3,806 bbl/Day [2011]
Oil Consumption: 231,000 bbl/Day [2011]
Proven Reserves: 1,940,000 bbl/Day [2011]

Partial Sources: Central Intelligence Agency

LOGISTICAL

Labor Force: 3,080,000 [2011]
Roadway Coverage: 18,290 km
Railway Coverage: 975 km

FINANCIAL (USD)

Defence Budget: $16,000,000,000 [2011]
Reserves of Foreign Exchange & Gold: $66,980,000,000 [2011]
Purchasing Power: $219,400,000,000 [2011]

GEOGRAPHIC

Waterways: 0 km
Coastline: 273 km
Square Land Area: 20,770 km
Shared Border: 1,017 km

NAVAL POWER

Total Navy Ships: 64
Merchant Marine Strength: 10 [2011]
Major Ports & Terminals: 4
Aircraft Carriers: 0 [2011]
Destroyers: 0 [2011]
Submarines: 3 [2011]
Frigates: 0 [2011]
Patrol Craft: 42 [2011]
Mine Warfare Craft: 0 [2011]
Amphibious Assault Craft: 0 [2011]

France
Service de Documentation Exterieure et de Contre-Espionage(DGSE).

DGSE was formed on 2 April, 1982. DGSE replaced the 'Service de Documentation Extérieure et de Contre-Espionnage' (SDECE) which had gone through many changes of name and function after the Second World War. Pierre Marion was its first director.

In 1942 the free French forces formed 'Central Bureau of Information and Action' (BCRA). BCRA was renamed 'General Directorate of Special Services' (DGSS) in 1943 and relocated to Algiers. All intelligence networks of the French resistance were incorporated into DGSS, which was renamed 'Directorate of Studies and Research'(DGER) on 6th November, 1944. The External Documentation and Counterespionage Service (SDECE) replaced DGER in 1946 to remove communist elements from the organization. SDECE was directly controlled by the Prime Minister.

France investigative philosophy emphasizes close relations and information sharing with other federal, state, local, and international law enforcement and intelligence agencies. A significant number of investigations are conducted in concert with other law enforcement agencies or as part of joint task forces. The language may be different but the French intelligence also works or coexists with the American intelligence and others.

France is a member of the UNO, and all the discussions in the meetings, that would lead to a peaceful situation. In the UNO, all the cats sit down together and deliberate on world issues irrespective of the different languages of each nation.

Do the members hear and understand each other?

The answer is YES but sometimes through listening electronic gadgets that translate the major language into other different languages. French president Mitterand did a lot for French government intelligence set up before president Jacque chirac took power and continued where he stopped, and in fact during the time of these two governments, peace reigned in all the French provinces, a lot of exchange programs between France and her African counterparts took place, and life moves on peacefully, modern equipments on information technology were introduced into most of the African French colonies to enhance easy contacts, gadgets like computers, internet and modern telephones were available in African French states. The African French citizens also travel to France to obtain good education and return back to their various countries in order to help the less privileged ones. In fact, President Chirac did a lot for the French people all over the world and also for the non French speaking people. The French intelligence under President Chirac was able to perform very well, without any territorial problem between neighboring countries, immigrants move from countries into France without any molestation. President Sarkozy came in, after to continue from where president Chirac stopped and he had full and total control of the French intelligence, the French intelligence has alliance or a joint task force with the American intelligence, in every world affair, this can be witnessed during the Libya crisis where the French cats under President Sarkozy, moved the missile bomber jet to destroy the nuclear plant in Libya while the American Military used only the ground forces during this crisis. What happened during this Libya crisis, I think happened also during the Iraq crisis, whereby most powerful nations of the world gathered together their military personnel to solve what they called a problem. President Sarkozy is not to be blamed so much, because I feel that he only played his own part.

During this moment the 2012 Olympic games was about some months ahead, and there was a rumour that the end of the world according to the Mayan calendar would be around this time of the Olympics, most people became afraid, and travellers decided not to go to London around December. The world intelligence communities, I think, were touched by the rumour, as no one knows what could happen, and all of a sudden the government of President Sarkozy was changed and President Hollande, the present leader of France took over the government. Up till now under President Hollande, there has been no problem and life continues as before. Most French African governments were happy with President Hollande for his good gesture towards them, and recently he helped the Malians to remove the Islamic rebels from disturbing the peace of the country, while these rebels were there, according to the Malians the radio programs were changed and the mode of living disturbed until France came to their rescue. The Malians danced and gave President Hollande a good welcome when he visited the place.

Strong cats and warriors are often known with boldness and violence, this is normal. But God who controls every situation, always do not go into violence at once, according to the episodes in the holy books, He makes peace first but when the right solution is not coming up then He applies violence, this is my own stand. For instance, the lord told Pharaoh several times to let the Israelites go out of the land of Egypt because of great suffering, but he refused and the lord applied violence and Pharaoh's warriors perished in the red sea. He warned the people of Sodom and Gomorrah to desist from their ways of life but they refused and he destroyed the land with violence. God would always make peace before turning to violence and he will always use his cats to send the warnings out and not straight away to violence. I love violence when the situation is not right and after peaceful warnings had failed to help the situation.

I am raising this issue, to see if the assassination of the Arab leaders can be stopped during any crisis in the Arab zone. If any Arab leader had stayed for a long time and the intelligence communities need a change, I feel that a peaceful step down can be affected first but when the leader involved refused then a violent change becomes inevitable. I know that a man that had enjoyed for many years and he is not poor, would always like to step down, no matter the situation, and a wicked ruler can always be removed too, at any time, if his conduct is against the ethics code of most intelligent communities, through this means of peaceful step down, without any problems. When there are inevitable violent situations, I feel that those involved can be removed. Destroying social amenities that cost billions of dollars to put into place, every time, is not the best but when violence is inevitable, the intelligence communities would always replace back the social amenities lost. Some groups of thinkers feel that any world leader that is not violent is weak, a vegetarian way of life but I think that this notion is wrong. For instance Presidents Bill Clinton, George Bush sr, and some others fought wars but never killed any Arab leader during their tenure of office, changes were made and life continued. They are intelligent and are not weak.

United Kingdom / Great Britain
Military Intelligence 5 (M15)
Military Intelligence 6 (M16) aka Secret Intelligence Service (SIS).These two intelligence organisations of United Kingdom, also operate like the American intelligence

On drug trafficking, they also determined that the most effective means of combating this crime is to use the enterprise theory of investigation, which focuses investigations and prosecutions on entire criminal enterprises rather than on individuals. Through this process, all aspects of the criminal operation can be identified. The theory supports not only the prosecution of the criminal enterprise, but also the seizure of the enterprise's assets and is intended to disrupt or dismantle entire criminal organizations. In the United Kingdom, the intelligence work closely with the Drug Enforcement Administration and through Organized Crime and Drug Enforcement Task Forces around the country. Other petty crimes are also taken care of, through special voluntary organisations and citizens. The citizens report any wrong doing or thing within the society to the police and the intelligence, this means that the people also assist their communities to be free of crime and peaceful and I think that the leaders in the communities sometimes too, give rewards to these good citizens, in terms of money or medals. They also occupy the minds of the youths with games, indoor and outdoor games and award to the winners, trophies.

Due to this reason, most of the youths that would have gone into crime, become better citizens, this type of occurrence can be witnessed in almost all the nations of the world

Netherlands
Algemene Inlichtingen- en Veiligheidsdienst (AIVD).

Today, the intelligence reports regularly go to the Senate Select Committee on Intelligence and the House Permanent Select Committee on Intelligence. The Intelligence Oversight Act and various Executive Orders dictated this structure.

The Agency reports also, regularly go to the Defense Subcommittees of the Appropriations Committees in both houses of Congress. Moreover, the Agency provides substantive briefings to the Senate Foreign Relations Committee, the House Committee on Foreign Affairs, and the Armed Services Committees in both bodies, as well as other committees and individual members. The intelligent cats in the Netherlands, also work very hard to protect their national security. In the Netherlands, life is normal like in most countries of Europe, visitors and immigrants to Holland move in and out without problems, meaning that the intelligence community is doing a good job to keep the security of the country. The intelligence cats in this country work the same way as the other cats all over the world.

Japanese Military Intelligence

It was evident that during the early stages of the Pacific War, Japan achieved a continuous spate of victories against the Allied forces in Southeast Asia and the western Pacific regions, and one of the key factors which contributed to the Imperial Army's success was the highly developed state of its intelligence capabilities.

Propaganda and subversive operations in Malaya and the Dutch East Indies were also carried out efficiently and the local inhabitants that acted as fifth-columnists and scouts for the Japanese invaders at the later stages of the Pacific War, as Japan's hold on the conquered territories crumbled against the allied counter offensive, and the errors and weaknesses of the Imperial Japanese Army's (IJA) intelligence became evident and during this period, the main shortcoming was the inability of the Japanese to conduct an objective assessment of the material and technological resources that were available to the US and the British forces, and a failure to understand the fighting capabilities of the forces that were ranged against the Imperial Army.

The problem of the Japanese military establishment occurred due to the fact that they followed a strategic culture which did little to encourage the rank and file to develop a realistic view of its opponents. The strength of their opponents they do not know and therefore it was difficult for them to win, Intelligence was one of many factors which determined the outcome of the Pacific War. The IJA lost mainly because it did not have enough capacity to subdue the Chinese on the Asiatic mainland, and also hold the American advance in the Pacific, in order to halt the British in Southeast Asia. At the same time, weak intelligence did lead the Japanese to embark on a venture for which they were ill-equipped to embark upon.

The preparedness, and the misperceptions of their enemies played an important part in preventing them from properly reforming their methods, the enemies of the Japanese, knew them well before the war started.

Strategic culture has been defined as 'a habit of behavior, a 'distinct and lasting set of beliefs [and] values' regarding the use of force, a set of basic assumptions concerning the threat posed by one's adversaries, and the accepted theories a nation holds on how it can confront the challenges. The term Strategic culture is used interchangeably with 'military culture', and the notion that strategy is linked to culture stems from the hypothesis that humans base their actions on the principles prevailing in their environment.

In short, it means that no matter how intelligent a cat may be, strategy plays a great role in actually getting answers to our problems.

In all the four areas, the Japanese cats performance was inadequate, mainly because its military establishment had what was a minimal experience in carrying out the intelligence activities that were necessary to give a successful war effort against a coalition of powerful enemies, over a protracted time period.

The value placed on intelligence activities, for example, on traditions and historical experience, and starting from its creation during the late nineteenth century, by the Imperial Army's culture was so low and the situation was largely a product of Japan's historical experience. Japan was inexperienced in key intelligence tasks such as gauging the mindset and capabilities of foreign powers. But today, the situation is a bit different because the Japanese cats are now having trainings in the Western world.

Military calculations were not based on facts, but the notion that Japan would eventually create a new East Asian order where it would play the dominant role in the world, overtook their minds.

But in an effort to promote public unity and establish a base of mass support, a national ideology proclaiming that Japan had the preordained right to become Asia's leading power was enacted...

The swift victories against China in 1894-95 and Russia in 1904-05 reinforced the Japanese faith in their ascendancy. Thus, a cornerstone of Japan's culture was an embedded belief that its people were a superior race, (Morgan, 2003, 64-65, 174) and this aspect reduced its ability to properly evaluate its rivals.

Japanese elite, during this moment, did not attach a high value to obtaining information on their opponents, the development of military intelligence had made minimal progress during the years prior to the outbreak of the Pacific War.

Directorate General of Intelligence (DGI) now Intelligence Directorate-The Cuban Intelligence.

Both the principal intelligence collection arms of the Cuban government which are the Directorate General of Intelligence (DGI) of Ministry of the Interior, and the Military Counterintelligence Department of the Ministry of Revolutionary Armed Forces is always associated with the Soviet and Russian intelligence services. This is probably due to the fact that these services are based upon the June 14, 1993 agreement on military cooperation between Russia and Cuba. The key Cuba organization responsible for foreign intelligence is the Intelligence Directorate (Direccion de Inteligencia), and before its name was changed in 1989, this body was long known as the General Intelligence Directorate (Direccion General de Inteligencia - DGI). Prior to the collapse of the Soviet Union, the DGI was closely aligned with and organised along the lines of the former Soviet Union's KGB, from which it also received training. During the Soviet era, foreign intelligence gained by either organization was occasionally shared. The (DGI) was established under the Ministry of the Interior (MININT) in 1961. The new agency included three Liberation Committees - for the Caribbean, Central America, and South America - collectively known as the Liberation Directorate (DL). In the early 1960's, the DL also was responsible for supporting liberation movements in Africa, including those who overthrew the government of Zanzibar in 1963. However Soviet economic pressure on Cuba in 1967-68 forced Castro to develop a more selective revolutionary strategy, and subordinate the DGI to the KGB. The KGB compelled Castro to replace its chief, Manuel Piñeiro, with José Méndez Cominches in 1969. The top cats know what the other cats are up to and this means that, if a cat is pushing a foreign policy that is detrimental to the survival of another one, there will always be a reaction. The DGI thereafter focused its efforts on collecting military, political and economic intelligence, with responsibility for supporting national liberation movements forming the new National Liberation Directorate (DLN), which was independent of the MININT. All the intelligence data collected helped in the formation of the new bodies like the DLN, the MININT and the DA. The DLN was subsequently reorganized into the America Department (DA), meaning that between America, Russia and Cuba, there is a connection which is invisible to the ordinary eyes, only the cats know all that goes on.

National Cats

As I feel, a natural cat sometimes go into hiding in order to catch its prey which is the mouse, for food, it goes into hiding in order to catch, it sounds interesting isn't it? in the real world, I think that the same thing happens, to the human beings but in a different form, some human beings turns into cats, go into their secret places to see what goes on in the communities, others who are not there with them are termed as below and must be dominated, they search for information of others in order to know what to do next. Nations also do the same, by spying on technological records and secrets of other nations. When the nation's spy, and see information that can cause problems, the leaders of such nations are summoned to UNO, FAO, UNESCO etc., for deliberations, depending on the real type of problem, whether educational or political or others, in order to find solutions to the problems. Without any noise, the people are aware of everything that is going on, because the cats are always on deck to inform the world of everything going on.

The cats in this category, can see and feel faster, stealing of technological records, is not a sin as it is a way of life to them, for example, financial, political and domestic information of others are sometimes stolen by powerful countries or are recorded for use in order to score political points, If the stolen records are patent ones backed by the law, the nations affected, always go to courts to demand for their rights. Through consultations, patent documents backed by the law can be given out to another country by the owner, if that country wanted such documents for her domestic use, without problems. Cats work together peacefully, share ideas and information for national development.

Sometimes too, the national cats sit down together in a meeting or forum, and in a neutral zone, to deliberate on issues that can bring social and financial help or peace; the leaders also exchange technological ideas and human manpower. It is a common thing that during most of these important meetings, pressmen are available to record and show to the world, all the activities of the proceedings and sometimes comments from notable rich people are sought as public opinions.

National cats do a lot of good to the world than evil, the people of different nations cross borders to live peacefully with each other without any problem, the immigration police and the national police of various nations also work peacefully together at the borders to make sure that things are done correctly and all are happy.

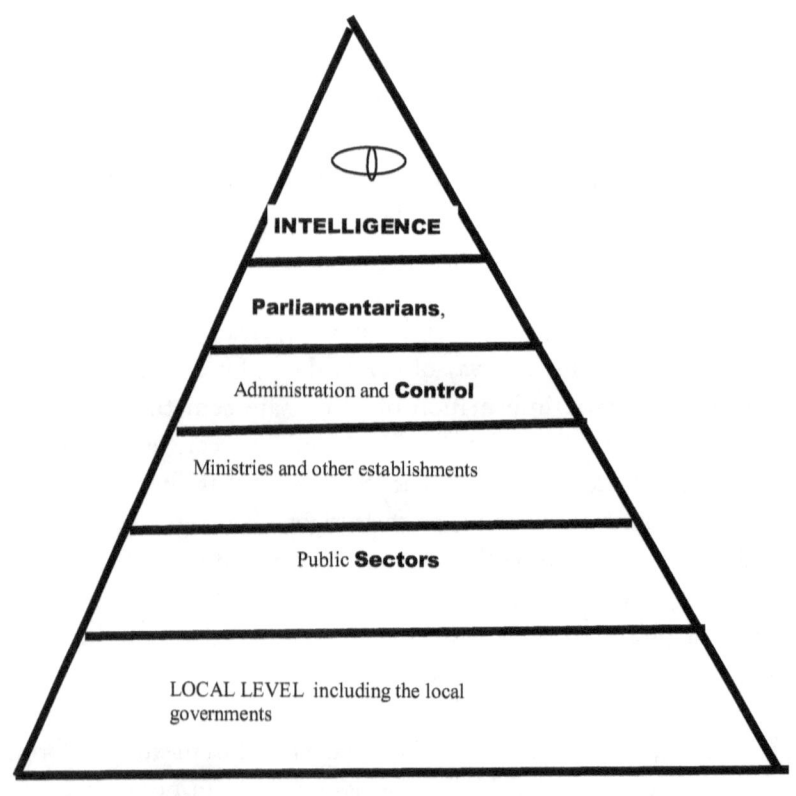

CHAPTER TWO

INTELLIGENCE WITH
OTHER CADRES OR LEVELS

Organisational cats

The top triangle has the INTELLIGENCE and in the intelligence, there, we can find the top most cats who know what goes on, every minute. The intelligence has the lords or lourdes, the judges, visible cats, Lawyers, invisible cats, Agents, and prominent people. It has the authority and responsibility to investigate specific crimes assigned to it and to provide other law enforcement agencies with cooperative services, such as fingerprint identification, laboratory examinations, and training. They also gathers, shares, and analyses intelligence—both to support its own investigations and those of its partners and to better understand and combat the security threats facing the country and the world at large.

Organisations like FBI, KGB, and others can be found at the top of the triangle also. Each country has its own secret organisation but I think that all can work together for world peace.

Anyway, the world has its own security organisations for the governance of all the nations of the world and they are, the UNO (United Nations) and the OAU(organisation of African unity) and they have their own security councils. Also there is the world court at Hague. In these security organisations, nations with their trained security men are represented and they understand each other and work together for the good of the whole world.

The second triangle, have cadres, which I summarised under six sub-headings

The human cats under this category can be found in the following groups-The military, the air force and the navy. They work, for the good of the nation that they belong to, by providing security and information as at when they are needed. The military provides the ground force, offensive or otherwise. The navy works on the great waters and seas. The air force provides, air tactics with the planes, aircrafts or jet fighters. All these three security arms of every nation provide useful services that ensure security and peace of the world at large.

The intelligence cadres

    a.   The Military OR the Parliamentarians.
    b.   Educational sectors, for example in the various Ministries, trade Unions, etc. OR the Administration and Control
    c.   Political circles, for example, in the various parties OR Ministries
    d.   Media/ TV—Journalists OR Public Sectors
    e.   Social sectors---film actors, dramatists, teachers and businessmen.
    f.   Local or Grassroot people

The military, for example has various divisions, and each division has cats in them, the cats under this category are well organised and they participate in the internal and external securities of their nations. They go to war, when it is necessary to go and when there is no war at hand, they protect their nations against invaders, the cats under this category, are at alert always, they assist during national disasters like hurricanes, floods and fire-disasters, they also rescue the people when it is necessary to do so. There are combatant soldiers and there are those trained to receive signals, also there are code-talkers.

Recruitments are made often and while the ordinary people are taken, the trained smart cats handle the new men and train them up, after training, the new people are distributed into all the existing divisions according to their areas of specialisation, those that want to change from one division to another due to new learning or new degrees are also allowed and they mix together. A good soldier does not disobey an order from the intelligence, the intelligence is above all, the type of food in the officers mess, the type of medicine in the hospitals, who is at the hospital, and when the salaries would be paid and why it must be paid earlier, all are known to the intelligence as things must be done orderly. The military cats have no time for nonsense, and duty is duty.

The educational sector with the ministries of education, have workers like the trade union leaders and the teachers. In the ministries, files of teachers are monitored so that life goes good, the trade union people also fight for their wards each time there is a problem. There are lots of cats in this sector too. Workers are being watched, leaders are also being monitored, probably for the reason that things should work properly. Teachers must work according to the laid down rules, and anyone who does not comply is warned, no one is free of being watched but while some watch for good, others watch for evil sake, some workers are frustrated by evil cats just because they want to score a point, if they want their men or women in some offices, they cause problems, so that their evil cats can enter the line, what type of problem? For example, they can tell the intelligence that the person involved is LANGSAM (Deutsch word) meaning that the person is too slow, he or she teaches two subjects in six hours out of the eight hours in a day; therefore the person goes to another place. No one can know a bad cat from the good one, by face but by his actions, he would be known immediately. In three months, a good worker can receive three KUNDIGUNG BRIEFE (sack letters) meaning that a good worker has changed work three times due to the action of the bad cats. The cats in one job place with the good worker watch and report every mistake of this worker to the boss; even pardonable mistakes are taken seriously, so that the worker can leave the job. The reason, for this action is for the worker to be frustrated and never survive, sometimes the bad cats create problems in the area where the worker works but the blame goes to the worker and he is sent away. This type of situation is actually very bad, and I think that the best thing is, for this worker to be told the duration of his employment and immediately the time is up, the worker finds another place, there is no need to witch-hunt or cause problem for a good worker simply because the big cat wants to frustrate him or her.

In the political circles, we have the politicians and the political parties. Under this category, the politicians are so vicious, in other words, great percentage of the cats here, are the bad ones, they give fine programs, to make the people vote for them, and the end refused to implement them. Some of the leaders spy the programs of others and confuse the people against those programs, this type of politics is common in less advanced nations of the world where many people are not educated and so, it is very easy to confuse the people. During politics, panic, tensions, and destruction of properties are common because opponents cause problems for each other. The political cats in one group with the same aims and ambition, work together and prevent the opponents from working properly. But in most advanced nations of the world, the cats understand each other and there is no opposition, a group splits into two and contest elections with each other, it is one family splitting into two and there is no danger but the fools will never know. In the political circles, most cats tell lies in order to survive and cats sometimes manipulate other cats in order to move ahead, on the road to the top, there are many mountains and it depends on who you know and where you belong to, there are cat-societies and there are secret societies, the intelligence knows at all times, who is more qualified to win in the advanced nations but in the less advanced nations, there are often cases of rigging or manipulations, which often results in riots and fights by opponents that have lost elections. During this moment, houses and shops are destroyed or burnt, public properties are destroyed and many innocent people lose their lives too.

Media/ TV- Journalists

Here, we can find expensive and brilliant cats, expensive and brilliant in the sense that, they are well trained to do the job; writing and reporting are part of their training. Their ability to search for information with modern software, and cameras coupled with computer training, is good. While some of them are good, others are evil depending on who controls them, they are fearless and it is only the court, that can save the members of the public from their hands, some of them work whole heartedly with no cover-up while others cover-up true news story after receiving bribes. The chief editors among them, are the ones that make sure that correct news are sent out, for readers to go through and the ones that the law does not permit are prevented from being published, some journalists too can edit the news items but they should still make the editor in chief to give the final approval before the story gets to the public. The cats here are well connected to the arms of government- the legislative, executive and the judiciary, they are known also, in the business circles. The ones that cover the parliamentary and senate proceedings are different from those that operate in the law courts and their presence makes everyone to behave normally in these arenas, they report what they have seen during their time of operation without any fear and they also conduct interviews, outside the parliaments and in the business circles. in order to sell their newspapers or magazines, the reporters with their cameras often go to commercial areas or business circles where the famous cats buys expensive articles and any action put up by these people is reported without fear, sometimes they take the photographs of people without notice and sometimes too, these famous cats demand for apologies which must be published for the whole people to see or read.

Social sectors

Most cats, here are social workers- plumbers, electricians, builders, clerks and messengers; they are mostly tools for the employers to use. They are mostly business people, and only few of them are well educated while the majority of the cats under this category are not so educated. The very educated ones manipulate the others and what goes on in every sector, is reported to those at the top. In the social sector, we also have famous educationists, mediamen, politicians, lawyers and other top people who are well educated and are known all over the world, some of them are top cats while others are just ordinary spies but they are mixed together, working towards the same goal. There may still be others who are very negative too.

Local or Grassroot cats-

Most cats at the local levels have little education and can be easily manipulated or controlled by the educated ones. LIES can be passed to them as facts and they will not verify the true situation. Once the people here believed something, it is difficult to erase it from their minds. Rumours spreading or backbiting is common with the local cats. They are easy to use, for protests and riots because always they think that they have been cheated.

Most local cats are very poor and they will do anything for getting the money, pasting of posters, distribution of papers and sharing of things among other local cats is a common activity. Most of them can be found in the bus garages, airports or commercial centres assisting the people to do one thing or the other, they know who is who in their environments. The local cats are mostly traders and musicians who have little or no education, to operate in the society, sometimes too, they are local killers or thugs who are used to cause confusion or fight at any moment. Whether big or small, a cat is a cat and any big cat that underrates the power of a small cat, always have problems because it is very difficult to know who is manipulating the small cat at any moment.

President Obama also had done a tremendous amount of work on the military, he recruits and trains the men and women, who have decided to make the military their career. He updates the stock by buying the new and modern equipments like aircrafts, ships and armoured tanks, for the use of the nation. I think that the United States of America manufactures some or all of the military equipments but they still need to buy from their own industry. The industry sells firearms, ammunitions and other military equipments to the other nations of the world that may need them.

The defence statistics are as follows;-

PERSONNEL

Total Population: 313,232,044 [2011]
Available Manpower: 145,212,012 [2011]
Fit for Service: 120,022,084 [2011]
Of Military Age: 4,217,412 [2011]
Active Military: 1,477,896 [2011]
Active Reserve: 1,458,500 [2011]

These records, shows how the American intelligence community care so much for their country's security system, the total population of soldiers as at 2011 is 313,232,044 people, the available manpower has 145,212,012 people, the people that are fit for service are 120,022,084 people, Of Military Age: 4,217,412 people, Active Military: 1,477,896. Active Reserve: 1,458,500 people. Useful services are introduced all the time, to save the people and the system, military recruitment is done at most time, to provide employment to the youths, these youths later undergo trainings and become fit to go on national assignments, millions of people work for the country's security service. While there are military personnel who work internally, there are others who work abroad or serve in the United Nations, all in the name of world peace. The United States spends a lot of money on the defence, apart from training, salaries of both workers and soldiers are paid on time, to encourage all the people in the military service to work fine. A lot of money is spent also on armaments, buying or building of armoured tanks, rifles, bullets and information gadgets like walkie talkie or telephones. Under this category, order is order; the military personnel receive order and carry it out and no questioning. They go on missions and the results are obtained, if a favourable result is obtained, all the soldiers involved are happy for a job well done and a documentation of how the war was fought and won is written down and kept, for historical purpose but if the nation had lost in any war fought, the reason why it had lost is also written down for future guidance or reference of the wild cats. The cats are sensitive, and they don't accept defeat, any defeat in any area, in the war front leads to reinforcements of more troops until success is achieved. The cats here wear special uniforms to make them different from the other set of workers and in the war fronts, they wear camouflaged clothes to hide them from the enemies and to make them perform smartly. Different types of vehicles are made use of, meaning that a lot of money is spent on buying of different sets of war vehicles and personal cars for the pleasure of the military cats, when there is no war at hand.

LAND ARMY

Total Land Weapons: 56,269
Tanks: 9,573 [2011]
APCs / IFVs: 26,653 [2011]
Towed Artillery: 2,163 [2011]
SPGs: 950 [2011]
MLRSs: 1,430 [2011]
Mortars: 7,500 [2011]
AT Weapons: 8,000 [2011]
AA Weapons: 2,106 [2011]
Logistical Vehicles: 267,247

The U.S. and Canada have done a pretty spectacular job of working together over the years despite a fair share of deep differences.

DARPA, the Air Force, NASA, Boeing, and Pratt & Whitney combine talent and energy on projects that the outcome is profound. The cats in these five companies join their resources together to advance the world forward in the field of aviation, new technologies come up through them and tests upon tests are affected before the real use of the planes is done. They make war and commercial planes.

The five companies are hoping that the case in test flight of the X-51 Waverider, an unmanned hypersonic scramjet that will tear through the sky at 4,000 miles per hour, will be successful as a super invention.

Though this test will see the X-51 dropped from beneath the wing of a B-52 at 50,000 feet over the Pacific, experts hope the technology could revolutionise air travel on everything from missiles, to manned aircraft.

The scramjet is supposed to be like comparing today's jet turbines to propeller driven aircraft, and is seen by many as the next evolutionary step in human flight.

Scramjet technology forces combustion to occur when airflow surpasses the speed of sound and hydrogen is injected into the flow, allowing for theoretical speeds of Mach 20.

That's what was hoped for during DARPA's Falcon Hypersonic Technology Vehicle 2 test flight. Unfortunately, that widely watched test ended in failure after the craft's skin peeled away from its body and the flight was terminated before any record breaking speeds could be reached.

The X-51 didn't fare much better during its previous test. The cats test most of the weapons in stock or in the armoury to ascertain their potentials, and when a machine is not yet standard for use, research works continue on it, until it is safe for use. Smart cats in the military and in the air force, work on special missions and they are well paid because they do specialised technical jobs to save humanity during great wars that must be fought at all cost

Hopefully the next test of X-51, after much improvement on it, would make this war machine, a super material in the hands of the users The success of this test, would put the cats under this mission, on a success list of world's best war and commercial planes technologists. The most powerful cats can be found here in the technological zone--the aeronautical engineers and the pilots.

Under the United States Military units, the total number of aircrafts as at 2011 is 18,234 and that of the helicopters, is 6,417 while the serviceable airport's total number is 15,097 also as at 2011. At the airports, a lot of workers are employed to work and see that everything goes on fine; the security aspect is taken care of, by the state and by the various security companies in the country. The airports and the immigration Police work hand in hand to see that everything in the military airports works perfectly, the commercial airports sometimes have military jets and planes landing on their tamacs but not all the time.

From a military point of view, the idea of hypersonic scramjet missiles is very important. Missiles and armouries are carefully guided by war commanders, and no missile is used by mistakes as there is order in the military, the soldiers in the Red Cross units take care of the combatant soldiers, when there is war and when there is no war, this unit has a lot of medical experts trained by the country to take care of the military personnel, there are also nurses to take care of the female soldiers and their male counterparts. All the soldiers live in the barracks except some high ranking officers who live outside the barracks. The military has a joint task effort with the international Red Cross community and sometimes they assist other nations during their time of problems.

But in civilian or military life, launching into the space, some of the military satellites for receiving and sending of signals is very common. Pointing heavy vehicles vertically up into the sky for launch or ready for launch, characterises military zones and behaviours and there are always soldiers guiding these equipments, 24 hours a day. Life in the military is sometimes very terrible, most especially during the war period when the soldiers have to go to the war fronts to defend their nations, always the nation with the most sophisticated weapons, wins.

The people found the Blackswift military aircraft exciting: while it was never intended to reach the Mach-25-equivalent speeds needed to achieve orbit, it was going to be a big step forward from the SR-71, previously the benchmark for sustained, practical-ish high-speed air breathing flight from a runway. Like its illustrious forebear, the Blackswift was to burn relatively normal JP-7 jet fuel rather than impractical, dangerous, bulky hydrogen; like the Blackbird, it was to take off and land on a runway and make no use of throwaway booster rockets to get up to ignition speed*.

The US Air Force, we learn from Aviation Week, has revived the aspiration for a reusable, hydrocarbon-fuelled runway hyper plane under the new name "High-Speed Reusable Flight Research Vehicle" (HSRFRV). Lovers of hyper planes will need to be patient, however, as the USAF intends to take a cautious path toward building the new Blackswift; it is not expected to fly until 2021, following years of trials and tests with WaveRider-derived missile-style weapon carriers.

CHRISTOPHER ABIODUN STEPHEN

These early tests – which might lead to a hypersonic scramjet missile that could fit into the weapons bay of a B-2 stealth bomber – would prove the main new technology required to beat the SR-71 Blackbird: that is, hydrocarbon-burning scramjets. The Blackbird was propelled down the runway and up to high speed by two hefty afterburning turbojets which were mounted inside cunning nacelles fitted with a retractable spike. At high supersonic speed, these nacelles functioned as scramjets and the turbojets nested within them were superseded, effectively acting as fuel injectors for the scramjet combustion chambers.

But a regular scramjet, even when travelling supersonically itself, slows down the flow of air through its combustion chamber to subsonic speed in order to avoid blowing out the flame. As speed climbs through the low Mach numbers this causes unacceptable levels of drag to build up, which is why the SR-71 couldn't beat Mach 3.5 or so.

Just like the United States Of America, Britain also votes a lot of money on defense, the leader at all times buy sophisticated weapons to guide the British nation and its territories, aircraft carriers and other fleets are also available with the British army and Navy. The British parliamentarians also see and approve most of the activities done in the country and after; proper records are made and kept in the archives. A cat knows what would happen in the future through inventions but the ordinary people would call these type of cats MESSIAHS just like most Christians call JESUS CHRIST. During the time of Christ, he was able to predict or do many things that will happen in the future, because he was a cat and today, the people call those things - MIRACLES. For example, HE said, in my father's house, there are many mansions and if it is not so, I would not have told you. This means that he saw the mansions that were there for many years and the things in them, which the ordinary people could not see.

In the technological fields, there are useful inventions coming up in the year 2021 and thereafter but as at the time of writing this book, we are in the year 2014, when this useful invention that will save the world comes, the people will say that, it is a miracle. What I am trying to say is that, if a man of God ten years ago, tell us that a flying machine that would be able to deliver cargo goods will be made and eventually in ten years, the drones come, the people might call this man of God a messiah but the truth is that he is just a cat.

The drone, because it is a flying robot, without a pilot, in my own opinion is a great modern technology which can be used in many ways. Apart from the fact that it can be used as a war technology, it can also be used to spy nations with nuclear armaments. It can also be used to distribute dangerous materials like chemicals or nuclear components which can cause contamination or pollution. Great credit should be given to the engineers, who have made this invention possible. While the rockets that go to the space have pilots, the drone has none.

On the drone, the advantages are more than the disadvantages

Advantages

1. The size of a drone is smaller when compared with a normal aeroplane.
2. No pilot.
3. Cost of training or employing a pilot is -zero cost.
4. Cost of maintenance may be low
5. If there is an accident on the way to a mission, no one dies.
6. A drone can be used to despatch letters or packages, fastly and effectively.

There are so many advantages, but I just limit it to six.

Disadvantages

1. If it is not well programmed, it can miss the target and perform a wrong mission.
2. It can be used to spread dangerous chemicals which can cause death.
3. It can be used to bomb any structure, anywhere.
4. It can also be used to bomb other nations; therefore it must not be sold to a crazy superpower national leader.

Oil Production: 9,056,000 bbl/Day [2011]
Oil Consumption: 18,690,000 bbl/Day [2011]
Proven Reserves: 19,120,000,000 bbl/Day [2011]

As at 2011, 9,056,000 barrels of oil was got per day while the consumption was 18,690,000 barrels per day, the proven reserve was 19,120,000 barrels per day.

The smart cats are used also, to guide the nation's wealth, the oil and gas production, mineral resources and mining. The mining is done and the report goes to the congress for analysis and ratification, after which it is stored in a safe place for further consultation. The workers under this category are trained by the state and only a few of them are employed to join the trained ones. In the mining fields, special types of uniforms are put on and various machines are used to separate the mineral from the ground. Those who grade the products, are different from those who market them, the quality control experts, make sure that the particular product mined is of a high quality that would bring good income for the state. Sometimes the country delegates some of the specialised jobs to some oil companies that have great knowledge to handle them, and to make the whole process faster. Every sale is reported to the congress for proper documentation. The oil or gas used for driving the military vehicles or jets is also accounted for, and the record also goes to the congress for documentation.

Other nations of the world, having oil and gas, have their daily data recorded and sometimes they sell out of their reserves to the United States, Canada and other countries that need to buy more oil and gas. In the African set up, most advanced countries, help in the mining process because of the costs of the highly technical equipments and staff, which these African countries cannot afford to buy or get but in the end, these advanced nations according to the deal or agreement made, get back their rewards. While some countries, can afford to pay for the services, others would like to give a certain percentage of the oil barrels as a deal in return for the services rendered. Oil and gas business is lucrative and many countries benefit from the use and the sales of these commodities.

THE MILITARY

The military guys all over the world are well paid and they are paid on time too. The army has a secretariat housing the civil and military workers who control the accounts department of the defence ministries, this secretariat, and deals with the payment of salaries, trainings and promotion of soldiers to various ranks. The workers in the secretariat are always mixture of civilians and soldiers and they do paper work most of the time. They work and receive promotions through recommendations by their bosses.

The labour force which includes both male and female officers as at 2011 is 154,900,000 people while the roadway coverage by the military is about 6,506,204 km. the railway coverage is about 226,427 km, Waterways: 41,009 km, Coastline: 19,924 km, Square Land Area: 9,826,675 km, and Shared Border: 12,034 km. The lands occupied by the military are often labelled as MILITARY ZONES and these lands always have the work offices, officer's mess for relaxation and living apartments, where the military men return to, after the day's job is done. Sometimes, sport and training areas are available too, and civilians cannot live in this environment, only visitors of the military men can enter this zone and they leave after visiting. The military cats are well taken care of, and they too are always battle ready when the need arises, early in the morning those that work in the offices move out to work, those that have trainings assemble and start to train while those with assignments in other areas, carry the military vehicles and move out on their journey. Every soldier has his time-table, knows his duty and all the work of each day is done accurately and quietly. Those that are new to the military duties are always informed by the coordinating officer for all the units, as to what they should do, and as per where they will go until they fully blend and understand their various divisions.

The financial capability of the United States of America on the defense of the nation as at 2011 is great, the Defense Budget: $692,000,000,000, the Reserves of Foreign Exchange & Gold: $150,000,000,000 and the purchasing power is $14,660,000,000,000. With this data, one can actually see that America does not play with the security of her citizens and also the security of the foreigners. The policemen, soldiers and other paramilitary men, all work and watch over the territories, to make sure that everything is alright, when there is a problem, the right action is taken by reporting to the next headquarter, that acts immediately.

Other nations of the world, train their military men in the United States or in other G7(seven most powerful nations in the world)nations, and after training the soldiers go back to serve their fatherlands. The less advanced countries also buy weapons from the United States of America and other G-7 nations. I think there is also a military joint task between the nations, in terms of exchange programs and training.

The military has its own hospitals with doctors and nurses, some of these workers are civilians while the rest are military trained medical personnel, these medical personnel often goes to the battlefronts to rescue soldiers that need help and in the cities, they also run ambulances to rescue the soldiers in the barracks or to help the families of soldiers in an emergency situation. In short there is division of labour in the military and there is also a joint task between the military and the navy. The naval officers attend the military hospitals together with their families and almost everyone under this category is healthy and happy.

NAVAL POWER

Total Navy Ships: 2,384
Merchant Marine Strength: 418 [2011]
Major Ports & Terminals: 21
Aircraft Carriers: 11 [2012]
Destroyers: 61 [2012]
Submarines: 71 [2012]
Frigates: 26 [2012]
Patrol Craft: 12 [2011]
Mine Warfare Craft: 14 [2012]
Amphibious Assault Craft: 31 [2012]

Despite aircraft carriers immense cost, the Navy believes there is no replacing a well-armed, aircraft equipped, sovereign piece of U.S. territory, powered by dual nuclear reactors.

Former Defense Secretary William Cohen was fond of saying that without "flattops" the U.S. has "less of a voice, less of an influence."

Perhaps, but there is another school of thought that questions the wisdom of floating something that is expensive within range of an attack that may send it to the bottom of the sea. Floating movable carriers can always move about on the sea within any range that the naval officers want and most of these carriers have standby aircrafts and jets on them, waiting for actions. The fleets are always placed in secret remote areas in the seas unknown to the people, but there are always officers with sensitive signal equipments to control the situation.

Carriers are likely here to stay as the U.S. works to replace its aging fleet with the new Ford class carriers and China builds up a fleet of its own. Every country has its own model of carriers, and the secrets of these technologies are well guided by each country involved in aircraft carrier making, the United States has one of the best aircrafts carriers in the world.

The British military strength can be compared also to that of the United States of America, and just like the American military force, the British army is also up to great task at any moment, recruitments and training are done as at when it is necessary and everything is in order. Under the British Prime Minister Margaret Thatcher, the military had a great strength with royal artilleries, regiments and infantries in place, guiding the British states and its territories. During civil disorders, in Britain or in Ireland, the military and the police often work together to help in quelling riots and protests, Thatcher was so good and in control during her days as the prime minister, John Major also did his best for Great Britain and I think, they were made or built by their party, The Conservative Party. Prime Minister Tony Blair, of the Labour Party continued where these two people stopped, recruiting and training more officers for the service of the nation. President George bush Jr convinced Prime Minister Tony Blair, to take part in the Iraq war, and after consulting the parliament, Tony Blair sent the British troops to fight in Iraq and they left Iraq when the parliament and the prime minister called them home, the American soldiers were the last set of people to leave Iraq. The British and American cats always see first and they also always lead the way while the others follow them, after a great convincion. I think the best cats are here in America and in Britain, since

I grew up, I have only seen the cats in these two nations leading others in world or European affairs, whether in war or otherwise. In the case of currency change also, all the countries of Europe changed their currencies to EURO but these two countries remained as they were, Britain still with the pound sterling despite the fact that they also belong to the European Union and America still with the dollar, this is incredible. The present British prime minister, David Cameron took over from Prime minister Tony Blair, and he builds on, putting more soldiers, policemen and other executives in the service of the British nation, and his country has been peaceful as it has been ever since.

STATISTICS
BRITISH ARMY STRENGTH

Strength of the Regular Army (mid 2012)

Armour	11 x Regiments
Royal Artillery	15 x Regiments (1)
Royal Engineers	12 x Regiments
Infantry	36 x Battalions (2)
Army Air Corps	5 x Regiments
Signals	12 x Regiments
Equipment Support	7 x Battalions (3)
Logistics	17 x Regiments
Medical Regiments/Field Hospitals	8 x Major Units (4)

Just like the United States Of America, Britain also votes a lot of money on defense, the leader at all times buy sophisticated weapons to guide the British nation and its territories, aircraft carriers and other fleets are also available with the British army and Navy. The British parliamentarians also see and approve most of the activities done in the country and after; proper records are made and kept in the archives. A cat knows what would happen in the future through inventions but the ordinary people would call these type of cats MESSIAHS just like most Christians call JESUS CHRIST. During the time of Christ, he was able to predict or do many things that will happen in the future, because he was a cat and today, the people call those things - MIRACLES. For example, HE said, in my father's house, there are many mansions and if it is not so, I would not have told you. This means that he saw the mansions that were there for many years and the things in them, which the ordinary people could not see.

In the technological fields, there are useful inventions coming up in the year 2021 and thereafter but as at the time of writing this book, we are in the year 2014, when this useful invention that will save the world comes, the people will say that, it is a miracle. What I am trying to say is that, if a man of God ten years ago, tell us that a flying machine that would be able to deliver cargo goods will be made and eventually in ten years, the drones come, the people might call this man of God a messiah but the truth is that he is just a cat.

On air force

Just like any other nation in the world, Britain has its own sets of aircrafts, the commercial ones, and the military aircrafts; there are also highly technical experts to handle them. These highly technical people also help in taking care of new inventions and skylon is one of them and they are partners in the existing companies that are noted for aircraft manufacturing in the world as a whole, and I think the aircraft itself is skylon. After building the planes, series of tests are done to make sure that they function perfectly-the engines, the fuel valves, the cables and others, there are tests pilots who are well trained to handle every situation.

There was an idea to build a huge, superjumbo-sized robot aeroplane which would mainly be filled with fuel tanks containing cryogenic liquid hydrogen and oxygen. Technically, it is fitted with radical SABRE engines, and the Skylon would make a rolling takeoff from a runway, leaving its oxygen tanks untouched to begin with and using the surrounding air to burn its fuel.

The Skylon could achieve a low orbit above Earth without any need to throw away expensive fuel tanks or boosters, delivering as much as ten tonnes of cargo into space. I feel that it is just like the drones that can be used to deliver cargo goods, and having completed delivery, Skylon would then re-enter the atmosphere, its novel huge-but-lightweight aeroshell resisting the heat, and come in to land on a runway just as the space shuttle does. But getting it ready for another mission would be comparatively trivial: it wouldn't need to be lifted and hoisted into a vertical position and strapped onto an enormous disposable launch stack of tanks and boosters before being moved to a launch pad very slowly on a mighty crawler vehicle. Rather the Skylon would simply be refuelled, reloaded and rolled back out onto the runway - taking off again in just two days, according to designers Reaction Engines Ltd.

Gentlemen, the anointed cats make research works, build and make life easy and possible, everyday for everybody. Without being told, new inventions, new things come up every day. For instance, cell phones, aircrafts, weapons, motorcars, bikes, wear shoes and so on, in Britain and all other countries of the world and at the same time. As I mentioned before, not all the cats are the same, while there are the good ones that make good things happen, there are also the bad ones, that feel that life is not worth to live and that everything should be destroyed, they look for good things and spoil them. They also scout for the good cats, blackmail and get them killed but the anointed ones of the lord, would always survive in the time of all these problems because they have the protection of the lord.

Continents, countries, states, or local communities, where we have a high percentage of good cats as compared to the bad ones, always develop faster and the environments look nice at all times but when the reverse is the case, there is no development and the environment is always dirty, it means that the cats in these dirty places are the bad ones, they are not in the good secret orders, their schools of thought told them that, there is no need to save or love their neighbours, and that doing business and gaining high profits by highly exploiting others is the answer to life, at the expense of others, they are also told that life is very short and there is no need to develop anything for the other people to come and enjoy(negative consciousness), I feel that this is a one way type of thinking but if someone have a two way type, he or she makes the money and still come back to use part of the money to develop the environment which he or she belongs to, for his people to enjoy, he or she can build hospitals, or schools or community roads, or use his knowledge to put in, new invention of aircraft or automobiles, putting good things where they should be and so on and so forth, therefore the happiness or goodness in any area depends on the percentage and the type of cats in such an area.

CHAPTER THREE

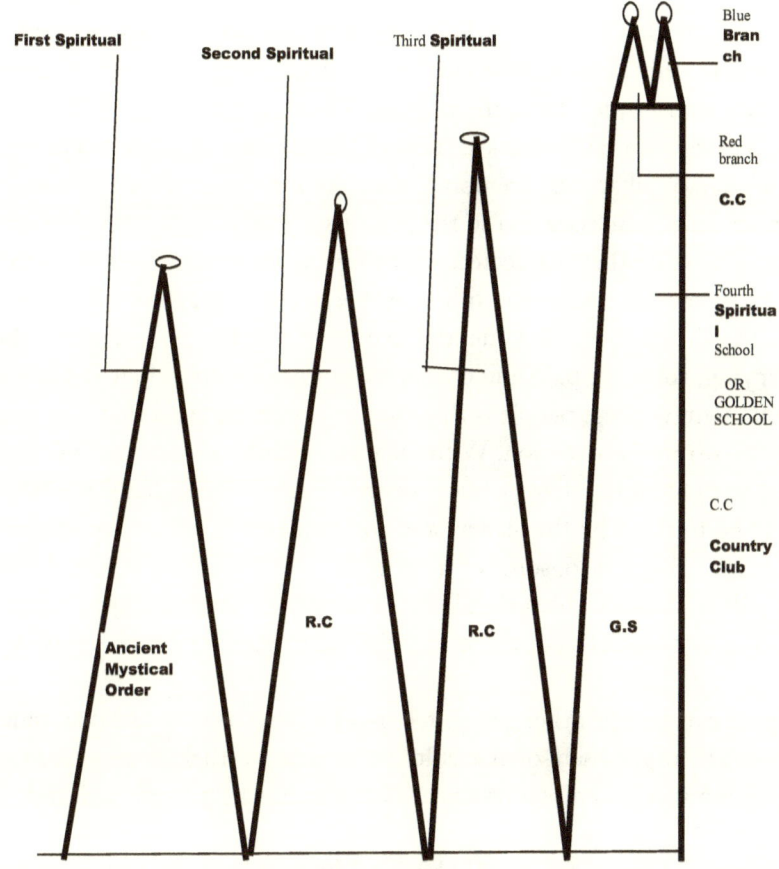

First Spiritual

Second Spiritual

Third Spiritual

Blue
**Bran
ch**

Red
branch

C.C

Fourth
**Spiritua
l**
School

OR
GOLDEN
SCHOOL

C.C

**Country
Club**

R.C

R.C

G.S

**Ancient
Mystical
Order**

MY GOLDEN JOURNEY

Social or Individual cats

Man is endowed with talents, for his own survival but most of the people in this category do not develop their talents, only to wake up, and plan evil and they are easy tools for those educated ones in the society to use, for protests and riots. Those that are educated and love to use their talents to help their fellow men are loved by few people, but they are always few, they are winners and they run stable government or administration, if they are managers because they are confident. Most cats, here are social workers- plumbers, electricians, builders, clerks and messengers; they are mostly tools for the employers to use.

They mostly don't have a political motive but can be manipulated by politicians, only an economic motive they have, they put their businesses and they are running them, the way they know. The majority of the people in this category are illiterates as most of them, don't have the professional knowledge of what they are doing, they are mostly employed by the few of them with businesses and so the fear of survival is always there to scare them and while they are scared, of losing the jobs, money or time, their ability to monitor what the other people are doing grows higher, they have the time to spy, backbite and expose wrongdoings, and while they are spying, some are paid and others are not paid as they do it as a hobby. The thought of these people is that they are oppressed and that they must fight to correct the situation. Without arms or ammunitions they go to the street to fight and destroy public properties, sometimes what they wanted are given to them by the leaders and sometimes too, what they ask for is difficult to give and so, some of them with their leaders are arrested, tried and jailed. Those of them that like to create confusions always end up in jail as in most societies of the world, their activities are not recognised.

They are cats but the other groups too may be cats, the wise cats manipulate the others to get their own results or to achieve their own aims, they employ, control and direct others until their aims have been achieved.

Few people in this category have business knowledge only, and sometimes what goes on, in the political arena, does not bother them, or sometimes it does, as some of them monitor the political situations of their area in relation to their businesses, by watching the proceedings on business matters weekly as they are conducted by the parliamentarians. These few cats, in order to operate well on their own, at times, steals the data of the people or companies, for their own use or for their employers, sometimes this attitude is not bad if the cats involved, are trying to bring up the economic standard of their companies to the highest standard of the top companies. For example, Dota is an anonymous member of a military-backed group of Chinese hackers notorious for stealing data from American companies.

According to Forbes, this group has likely broken into computer systems owned by Coca Cola security tech firm RSA, and energy company Schneider Electric.

But the fact that security firm Mandiant was able to screen-capture Dota in action. It's pretty compelling evidence, showing the hacker registering a new email address (he even provides his phone number for the SMS verification), breaking into victim computers, and stealing their data.

Also the Directors or Managers that are cats themselves sometimes put representatives in various government in order to know what goes on there, every moment of the day, those in the political arena also sometimes put representatives in the business circles, to know who is who in the business arena, dominating or at the top of the chart as the best Director. When new inventions or formulas are out, the Directors know quickly because they are represented in most organised set up.

This is the real world for you and me, the cats in the political arena are more powerful than the other ones but one cat can be in all the sectors, be it economic, social, geographical or political, and he is capable of being a businessman at the same time, and a politician with representatives running the businesses while he is at the top watching over everything, after all what is new in the world of today.

The cats in this category, have no problems putting their businesses anywhere in the community that they belonged to, and in their hiding places, they see who is who in the community and this is why the individual cats are very dangerous sometimes, because they often push the competitors away and out of business, in case the cats involved are not knowledge-able enough to compete well with them. Cats with great business and economic knowledge are able to monitor progress and bring up their companies economic standard to match or surpass the existing growth standard to some extent. To transport their products to buyers or to the neighbouring country, or to get the best brains for their works, or get the loans, and manipulate others, are very easy tasks for the few cats who know what to do. Those that want to be in the business circles, after leaving the school finally, first work with one establishment before setting up their own, and as cats, the knowledge gained from the first place of work is normally put into use in the new establishments, formed later on. In any industrial set-up, they sometimes form joint task effort with other cats, in order to bring about efficiency.

Where the individual cat wants to put the business, or how many people he needs or the source of the capital to start with, is always the first priority and after all these had been done, he then goes about the training of his staff. The individual cat is the sole owner of his business, he uses his workers and he makes his profits, he can turn his business into a joint stock one by bringing into the business, other business executives or partners, to join him. What goes on in the industry of his specialisation is his business, and his workers or representatives report to him or sometimes through the internet, he himself gathers the data or the information by himself, for instance, information on profits, new business software and the leading entrepreneur or capitalist in the area are top priorities on his agenda.

Most individual cats turn into cats for survival sake and I think that this is normal. The individual cat knows when to go for loans or to expand his business under a favourable economic situation and he does so when the demand for his products, is high and the profits keep rising high. More branches of his company and the members of staff are needed during the expansion time, and he also know which of the banks would give the exact amount of loans that he will need, an individual cat who is a businessman can also be a politician and combining the two activities, is very easy for some while it is difficult for others but the person who can combine the two, is more known and acceptable to almost everyone in the society, he has an income from the state as at the end of each month and at the same time, his business brings to him some amount of money also and every time.

This type of individual cat because of his political activities is known in the geographical regions by everyone, and sometimes, if he is an agent of the FBI or CIA, it is difficult to detect. When the world is in a peaceful situation at most times, it is as a result of these type of individual cats, in the midst of the people, they see what is wrong and they inform the right establishment, to correct the problem at once but most of us wake up to find everywhere looking brilliant without knowing how it had happened. The individual smart cats do a lot of good things in the society than evil and without them, sometimes the lazy public workers can do and undo, for instance, the workers can leave or abandon projects to be finished in two years, for more than four years, public transport drivers, may refuse to keep to time or the officers may abuse their positions by not doing the right thing, financial institutions may charge fees or interests, different from the fixed ones by the government, if there are no sets of people, like these ones, watching and reporting, therefore things would not be done properly and there will be problems every time. This is the reason why the presence of the smart ones is necessary among us.

The individual cats in the imports and exports businesses, also do a lot of good jobs, by making sure that the real imported goods enter into each country and with the correct papers showing the import taxes paid by the companies, the same thing happens to the exported goods that goes out of each country and the amount of money made by the country involved in the businesses, all the papers checked and confirmed as correct by these cats. They also make sure that there is no fraud made by the companies' executives and the government workers. Apart from these sets of individual cats, the custom officials whose duty is to check all the papers connected with import and export duties, also crosscheck all the work done, to be sure there are no errors in the income chart of the country involved, and the paper is then sent to the senate for approval and records. This is how the individual cat working for himself, also work for the state, the knowledge he gains from government work is put to work in his private business. There are some individual cats that have never worked for the government and they feel happy working alone and making the profit, sometimes we call them the capitalists because they own the big industries and take most of the risks.

Some individual cats, work for their clubs, write the club's journals and inform the members of meetings time, these cats know everything that goes on, in their clubs and in the nearby social clubs, they know the rich people and those that are not so rich in most societies, in which they operate. They sometimes make joint task efforts possible between their clubs and other clubs, and they put social structures into places within the communities, structures like train, tram, or bus-stop stations, with sheds or shelters against rain, snow or sunshine, the stations are always provided with iron seats and painted neatly to help the people to wait patiently for the arrival of their means of transportation, for instance, bus, tram or train.

The cats in the clubs also help in the building of schools, sometimes they donate buildings to the needy people like the motherless babies or the handicapped people, some cats individually donate money to charitable homes, or sponsor brilliant but poor kid`s education.

A lot of good work is done by the good individual cats towards their people, communities and their nations but this is not to say that there are no bad individual cats, they are also available but in a good society, their number is so small and in a bad society, their number is high, and they do all sorts of criminal activities, with their companies, by bringing into the countries a lot of fake things like drugs or fake articles in order to make millions of dollars if undetected, they also participate in credit card frauds, import and export frauds, fake cheques or fake money, printing of fake currencies or fake import and export licenses, all in the name of economic survival and at the end of the year, millions of dollars are made by some of these individual cats. If these fake individuals made their money un-noticed, they are happy because they have made tax-free money but any time the frauds are detected, the people involved are always charged to court and if found guilty, must return back the money acquired through these fraudulent means or go to jail, if unable to do so, the state also publish the lists of fraudulent companies and the names of their directors and place the information in the national newspapers and magazines, therefore when the people have the information, they guide their workers from dealing with such companies and their directors.

But, not every business director like to be fraudulent because of the jail terms involved, those that have done well, without fraud are always rewarded by the state, through awards of certificates of efficiency or good quality control or of merit with cash rewards attached, this is done in the open with television cameras recording and showing the news to the people, this is one of the ways by which the state encourage the individual business cats to be honest. When a company is rewarded by a nation and the ceremony had been performed, the director of such a company often do the same thing within the company by gathering the workers together in a party, to celebrate the success of the company in their community, where other companies are also trying to survive and compete with them. During such ceremony, food and drinks are served while the director reads out the past activities of the company, stating the performances of each section or department and at the same time congratulating the leaders or the head of such departments. Distribution of certificates or cash awards to the various heads of the departments and the workers under them is always the last on the agenda and it is done, after food had been eaten and drinks taken. This way of showing gratitude to workers is common everywhere in the world and the company certificate of excellence is always displayed on the wall in the premises so that all the workers would be happy seeing it.

It is always a happy moment in the life of the workers and their families, and this grateful attitude of the director makes the workers to put in their best to work at all times and when eventually they are at home with their families, their children are glad seeing their parents being so honoured by the company they work for. In this way, companies grow and expand and the effect of their growth affects the nation's economy, which also rises up to affect the world's economy, therefore we can all see that the activity of the cats, boils down towards saving everyone and that it is a sort of chain reaction.

SECURITY

The power of human cats is so great and enormous, to the extent that if checks and balances are not put to it, breaking of laws and disorderliness could always occur, and because there are laws and checks, this is the reason why everyone is careful not to misbehave in the society. A human cat can go jail, if he or she misbehaves by committing crimes but if he or she is a big cat, big in the sense that he or she is or was, a president, or a governor, or a family member of presidents or governors, then he or she may be above the law and does not go jail, this is the reason why other lesser human cats should be cautious, in dealing with any situation. Sometimes some rude human cats lose their lives in action unknowingly because they do certain criminal activities just for the reason that others too have been doing them. Cats that are not strong enough should not copy the bad behaviours of the other cats otherwise they end up in jail. For instance, a president is importing illegal things and because you are a cat who works in the customs, you want to do the same thing, it is easy for you to go to jail but the president will never go to jail because of the immunity he has got.

I am talking about capital crimes like fraud, damaging of public properties, killing of people, robbing of banks, illegal importation or illegal importation of harmful things into the nation and so on, I am not talking about small problems like fighting on the street or unauthorised parking of cars in some areas or an abuse of authority and others. The big cats can commit all these crimes, if they want and nothing would happen, because they are the LAW.

The readers of this book may say that, the law supposed to be the law and that no one should be above it. Yes, it should be so and even the constitutions, said it should be so but the world is sometimes according to the story of ANIMAL FARM which says that all animals are equal but some are more equal than the others. In other words, I am saying that anyone who takes the president of his nation, who is the biggest cat, to court, has only gone to the court to waste his time and money because the man may be everything in his country, but he looks simple and quiet, therefore lesser cats should not underrate the power of any big cat. While there are other big cats in the background and are INVISIBLE, I think that the most powerful VISIBLE cats in the world today are seven in number and they are the G-7, you know them and I don't need to mention the G-7 nations, their decisions and actions are watched every minute and analysed to avert world wars and I think that they are wisely chosen too. The actions of these cats must be carried out, once the two thirds of them countersign a decision but normally the seven members of this group always support each decision they all made together. Most of the dangerous decisions they make, are done in secret.

To discuss this issue of security, I have four divisions, namely (a) World security (b) National security (c) State security (d) Individual security.

For the world security, nations always come together or are represented in forums or in organisations, for example, the UNO, NATO, OAU, FAO and so on, to discuss issues affecting each other and how to resolve those issues amicably without further bringing new problems. The leaders of each nation may be present in the meetings or they may send a delegate each to represent them, if they are not chanced to be present physically and after a matter has been resolved, it is documented and signed, and each nation have a copy of the paper. In this way there is no problem coming to the citizens of these nations because a joint task has been made to solve all the problems that they may encounter. Most problems are mainly on immigration or passports but sometimes it can be economic, social or criminal and there are agencies that are already there to solve these problems. Under this system, there are checks and balances to power, and there is no absolute power usage, that is, a nation cannot do as she wants but must follow the laid down rules by all the nations, if there is a problem. For the world security, no nation can be above the law and if a nation breaks the joint made laws, such a nation can be punished with a fine of money in cash or barred from certain activities, a nation cannot go to jail like the humans.

On national security, each nation decides on what to do when there is problem but also under this system, there are checks and balances, the two federal houses of the parliament, the legislature and the senate, write the bills and the president who is the leader signs the bills into laws. The executive arm makes sure that the law works while the judiciary punish the offenders. Each arm is independent, the judicial arm cannot make the laws and the parliament also cannot punish offenders, the executive arms cannot also do the work of both the parliament and the judiciary, only to carry out the laws and make them to work. Under a normal circumstance, no one is above the law but in practice if a powerful leader commits a crime, he is always free because he is the LAW, he puts the people in all the arms of government and nobody can antagonise him, the rest people can go to jail, if they commit crimes. Also a president can pardon a person and that person will not go to jail.

On the state security, the system is the same; here we have state houses of parliament, state executive arm and the state judiciary. It is the governor that signs the bills into laws and there are checks and balances and no one can take the law into his hands. But when a clause or a part of the state's law contradicts that of the federal law, the federal law is used because the constitution stated so. The governor, also in his state is above the law because he is the LAW there, but in practice, if he is not in good terms with his president, his president can pull his legs, if he commits, crimes with capital punishments, by taking him to the highest court of the land which is the supreme court and if there is immunity on his position, he as a governor, only pays fines, If found guilty, he does not go to jail. But the leader had tarnished the image of the governor by even taking him to the court to make the people to know about all the atrocities he had committed.

The people in the state are free to do all things except committing civil or criminal problems otherwise they go to jail.

On individual security, the security of the world, that of the nations, and also that of the states, is the security of an individual, it is like a chain reaction, if the world is peaceful, it means that most nations of the world are also peaceful, and if the nations are peaceful, it also means that the states under the nations are peaceful. In total, if everywhere is peaceful, then an individual has no problem, the checks and balances formula is working with everyone. An individual can be a big cat or a lesser one, he or she can be in the employment of the nation or the state and he or she can also be a self-employed human cat, while running his or her businesses, he or she can also be in the federal service employment, and other cats run the businesses on his or her behalf. There are economic, social and political securities for this individual cat, he knows those that are worthy in every situation and he is powerful.

He or she may be good or bad, if he is bad, apart from his bad actions, the thoughts that what happens in other nations or other regions is not his or her concern or problem, always come to his mind. He believes always that as long as, his or her area is fine, other places can go to hell, but a bad cat forgets that any problem in one area can spread to the other causing a lot of harms, whether economic, political or otherwise, therefore a good cat should let the problems of everywhere be his or her concern so that a situation like Japan bombing the Americans and the Americans retaliating by bombing Hiroshima and Nagasaki does not reoccur. Israel, Iran and Syria should watch their actions, and I think that the United Nations too, should watch closely these three nations, so that the leaders don't start another world war because the region having these nations is characterised with uprising and political problems and some of these nations have nuclear weapons.

An individual cat that is religious, is always seen in his church donating part of his money to the orphans and to the charitable homes, he also gives money towards the building of the temples, which are the houses of the lord, where everyone can enter and pray. Some of them also hold good positions in the church and they do most of the church satellite and communication installations that make the whole people to receive the programs, at the right time. They are very helpful in the society too.

CHAPTER FOUR

Geographical and religious cats

These sets of cats are found in the Christian, Hindu, Buddha, and Muslim religions and these religions are located in the various regions and continents of the world. In the American continents, we have America and Canada in the north while the South America consists of the Latin countries, countries that are known to speak the Spanish language. In these American continents, the dominant religion is Christianity which is known with churches and temples, other religions are present too but they are not so common and this means that most of the religious cats in this area are Christians.

In the African continent, there are all the religions named above, Christian, Hindu, Buddha and Muslim religions; also there are African traditional religions. All these religions have their cats and a cat can be in more than one religion if he or she likes to be, in multiple religions, the mosques are known with the Muslims and the churches with the Christians while the traditional worshippers have objects which represent their gods.

Under the traditional system of worship in Africa, we have the OGUN, OSUN and others, the OGUN worshippers worship the iron and they do so by pouring palm oil, palm wine on the iron, they also break kolanuts and use palm leaves during their worship, as their belief is that, anything made of iron is powerful and must be respected, objects like cars, aeroplanes, iron chairs, cutlasses and other agricultural tools made of iron are treated as objects of great importance and there is a belief that life is worthless without iron. The cats under this category are mostly illiterates consisting of men, women, and children, and they wear traditional attires during their celebrations. The educated ones in their midst are very few and they guide the rest members of the group during their worship, to do the right thing. It is very easy for these few ones too, to tell lies and manipulate the rest cats in the group because their opinions are respected always.

The cats in the OSUN tradition worship the rivers and their belief is that without the rivers, there is no existence. They wear whites during their celebrations and the group consists of men, women and children also. There are also few educated ones among them. Some of the OSUN and OGUN worshippers inherited the tradition from their illiterate parents but as soon as they get converted into Christianity, they confess and never return to the old tradition but these days we still have some too that are still in the old tradition but still, they are Christians, as their names have not changed into new Christian names. The cats in the traditional worship are very few in numbers and traditionally they are very powerful and they fight with black power any time they are offended. Majority of the traditional cats don't believe in the existence of God.

IN EUROPE

The Christians are many and everyone goes to the church that pleases him or her and while other religions are available, the worshippers are not so many like the Christians.

In the European continent, the dominant religion is Christianity and this is why we can find many churches and temples here, the Muslim religion also, is available but the worshippers are not many in Europe. Various other religions are also here but in the minority.

In the Asia continent, Hindu and Buddha religions are the dominant ones in this area and the religious cats under this category have their temples just as the Christians have and the worshippers consist of men, women and also the children. Churches are available too. These religions are known with the Indians, Koreans and the Japanese.

In the Middle east, the dominant religion is Islam and the worshippers have so many mosques in the region.

Israel is a Christian nation with a lot of Christians but the Muslims are also living there but their population is low when we compare it with the population of Christians. Other religions are also available in Israel.

In the Christian community, we can find a lot of churches and just to name a few of them, I have the church of Jesus Christ of Latter Day Saints, the catholic church, the celestial church, the Methodist church, Jehovah Witnesses and the Baptist church. All the Christians under this group believe in the existence of one God and his son Jesus Christ. But the doctrines and the mode of dressing in these various churches are not the same. Before we can talk about the cats in the Christian community, it is proper to know the churches and what they stand for.

I was born into the catholic church and I attended this church for many years before another church was introduced to me by some groups of elders of the church of Jesus Christ of latter day saints, I was given three religious books together with the bible to go through, the book of Mormons, the pearls of great price and the doctrines and covenants. I met these elders in Spain, Europe and as at that time I was only with the bible, it was fascinating to find other three books talking exactly like the bible and revealing many spiritual information. The church pamphlets gave me the church website address in the internet, I crosschecked and found that the church is great and noble, I was convinced and I joined but I am still a catholic. Any place, I visit, I attend both the Catholic Church and the Church of Jesus Christ of Latter-day Saints. Catholics have 6, 7, 8, 9, 10, and 11 o'clock mass or service but the time varies with countries while the Mormons have 9 and 11 o'clock service only, on Sundays. I was baptised into the two churches, I enjoy being in the two places every Sunday but at different times, and this is how I came about with my RED and BLUE outfit, if I wear my red outfit without the blue one, I always feel uncomfortable until I put the blue on top and I believe that I am the two churches.

There are many people, who are spiritual and they have purified thoughts because of the sacred truths that they know, they are rich, and are very happy but if Buddhism says that happiness does not exist, I think that this is a mistake, there are many people in the world today who are very rich, and have never suffered before but are conscious, and with purified thoughts, they also have children, good wives, they live good. For example, the world's richest billionaires, who have children that had never worked before and they are rich because those children inherited the wealth of their parents. This set of people is many in the Christian organisations and most of them donate part of their money to the poor. The best cats in the world are among the Christian and the Muslim folks and to me; anyone who suffers himself or herself for purification purpose is not a good cat. For self purification, Christians and Muslims always observe fasting and prayers, and I don't think that this is a form of sufferings. Anyway, a person can be a Buddhist following the way of Buddha but still having the beliefs of Christ just like I am a Christian but I still have the knowledge and the beliefs of the other religions, the beliefs only, because I cannot worship stones or bow down in the front of images, and if I do, I am just fooling the people doing so. Immediately a person starts to worship stones then he is not Christ-like, and he cannot be saved until he had repented. Therefore someone who changed from his old ways to the way of Christ through repentance can surely be saved. People can be saved, even one minute before they die if they repent, and I feel that this is the reason why the priest is asked to preach to or pray for a dying person before he or she finally dies, so that the soul can go to God.

In the catholic church, some non-members think that the Catholics worship the images of Mary, Joseph and Christ by kneeling down in their front to ask for favours but the answer is NO. I think that places around these images are made very comfortable for the people to pray and it is like someone sitting down with the family of Christ and asking for favour and with great belief, such favours are always granted to those who ask for them. Most of the religious cats in the Catholic Church are also business people who give their money to charitable and motherless babies homes, they help the less fortunate members among them too. The head of the Catholic Church is called the POPE and the elect as I think, has the right to stay for a longer period as the church decides unless he wants to resign. The present pope Benedict 16, Ratzinger, from Deutschland, decided to resign due to old age and a new pope had been elected, his name is Jorge Mario Bergoglio--Franciscu and he is from Argentina. He was elected by 115 cardinals from all over the world, in the month of March, and in the year 2013.

The beliefs and the doctrines of the Methodist, Baptist and the other churches are also a bit similar to those of the latter day saints and the Catholics but the mode of dressing of the priests, is different. While the Mormons have white shirt over black trousers, others have their own like the academic gowns but of different colours of white, red, green.

Baptist priests sometimes use collars round their necks during church services. But only the Mormons have many temples around the world for the performance of sacred ordinances.

Do the churches have cats like the other establishments?

I think the answer is YES, and in the olden days, and sometimes now. The Roman kings and other kings have knights that are known to have alliance with the Catholic Church and most times, these knights are present in the church during the service to represent the kings. As at this period, the Catholic Church also have other cats in the church whose duty is to inform the king of what is happening in the church, state or in the country. Catholic churches are known to have a lot of societies, for instance, Saint James society, Franciscan society, Saint Joseph society, Immaculate Concepcion society and Holy Mary society and so on. The activity of the religious cats, is to know what each society is up to, vis a vis the activities, who and who is a member, the status, the meeting periods and what each member says during the meeting time. The king or the leader of the church is like God to the Catholics because after he has heard the pleas of the members of the church, he solves the problems right away and those problems that he cannot solve, he tries to solicit the help of governor of the land who tries to solve them. Religious cats are very powerful because they also make joint task efforts with the state and country, and the bishop with overall ruler (the pope) representing the kings each time they are out for meetings. It is common to see the religious cats influencing or favouring those that have religious beliefs to capture power, even in a land that does not practice Christianity while the others with different religious beliefs, follow these favoured cats and I think that this is correct. Among any group, there are invisible cats, whether we like it or not and they are there for a particular reason which is also secret. A cat or some groups of cats, with the same skin colour can blend with the people of another country whose people are in a great slumber and without consciousness, and after take the country away from them. If we sleep off and unaware, we may fall. Cats that have the same beliefs can unite with the administrators of a country, a company and a group and survive as long as they are one and in one accord. When there is no unity, there is always problem and separation occurs.

The lord Himself told His anointed to watch and pray, so that there will be no fall and so that the devil does not conquer them- Mark 13 verses 35, 36 and 37. To prevent injustice in the society, the right cats must be at the right positions at the right time because the agents of the devils too, do not rest, as they always sow seeds of discord and confusion in order to bring injustice to reign in the society. For example in the parable of the sower, in the bible, the devilish cat planted weeds among the crops without the knowledge of the owner, it was when the crops grew up with the weeds together, that the owner detected that someone had planted thorns among the crops, in order to kill the real crops, and so he started removing the thorns. Sometimes the agents of the devils also spy and destroy files that would make life worthwhile when they are in the midst of the good cats and the bible said that the devil has only come to spy and destroy, therefore we should all watch and pray.

The bible also said that the land is the lords and everything therein, showing that both the devils and the anointed are also the instruments of the lord, therefore I think that sometimes too, the lord can use the bad ones to make the anointed to work or walk straight and do as He had commanded, meaning that bad cats can save the good ones sometimes, according to the plan of salvation. For example, Judas betrayed Jesus Christ and also Peter denied Jesus Christ, all for the good of the world, if the betrayer and the denial didn't happen, then God would have been called a liar because He promised that these things must happen at the appointed time and they did happen.

I think that the lord put the bad cats and he also put the good ones, to guide His own through in the moments of difficulties, the bad cats know the voice of the lords and obey each time, they hear it. There is light and there is darkness but the lord knows them all.

The worldly bad cats and the wolves consume the sheep and the goats but the ones for the lord, they can never consume because the lord protects them, for His use 1st Peter 3 verse 12 and 13

These churches which are the leading ones can be found in most continents of the world, the American continents, Asia, European and African continents.

In this book, I like to use the Catholic Church and the church of Jesus Christ of latter day saints as typical examples because they are the biggest, and the most organised.

The church of Jesus Christ of latter-day saints has the headquarter of the church in Salt Lake City, in the United States and the branches and the wards are also all over the land of America. Also in America, the Catholic Church is much organised with many branches but the headquarter is in ROME. It is from the headquarters of these two churches that, instructions flow to the branches, and the members are happy to worship every Sundays and other worship days, in every land of the world.

The temples are always built in strategic harmonious zones, for the performance of sacred ordinances and the Mormon temples were built according to this harmonious state, with flowers and beautiful trees around, the earth is always covered with grasses and every time they are trimmed beautifully, to make the environment, look green.

I am very happy that I know these two churches well and I would like the lords to come into my country through me, to save the whole people who think that they are in the light but are in total darkness. It is when, the spiritual light is beamed over my nation that the total darkness disappears, and I pray that the lords should use me to put more latter day churches and temples, all over the lands of my nation. The Masonic temples which will be under the supervision of the American and German great masons, are already existing and showing the people the real way to harmony. Only a true seeker can know that they are there. The catholic churches are already in large number and in strategic locations, but the only thing remaining is to maintain them well, so that they will continue to do the good work of the lord. Hunger disappears; great technologies come up like in Europe and South Africa and everyone knowing his or her right without begging to survive. The cities also having jet trains, and other good means of transportation systems like most developed nations of the world and nobody is in rags as it is common these days. The nuclear energy centre should also be made available to supply electricity to every corner of my country-NIGERIA. The lords have cats that can do it.

Road, train, tram links from my country to other countries, so that medication, food and other supplies circulates and everyone is happy.

Travellers coming for temple meetings or business, from other nations, to my land, should make their trips easily without accidents on their way. Joint task efforts between the Europeans and my countrymen should also be done without fear. All these can be done if the lords want them, through me by bringing the wise cats to work with me without any mafia thoughts, through exchange programs in a very organised form.

I as a cat like to operate on a solid foundation with my PLAN OF HAPPINESS on my table, and under seven platforms and each platform represented in whatever I do, if the lords use me.

For instance, in meetings, in working zone and in my business.

Apart from the other ones, in which the seven (7) must be present all over the nation, I would still like to have two latter day saints temples built, one in the north and the other in the south catholic churches are already many but only maintenance is required.

seven special hospitals.
five or three foreign television stations.
seven banks.
seven national libraries
seven national B Petroleum stations
seven Bakeries.
seven bookshops.
seven supermarkets.
seven modern prisons- inmates learn trades inside and work after.
seven BRY societies.
seven health insurance companies-health-cards- payment of fees when working/ old people - no payment.
Restaurants/ Clothing centre -everywhere but with the 7 cats in control.-No Hunger and no one in RAGS.
Top 7 executives in the states and 7 in the centre.

Underground sewage and dirty water tunnels leading to the sea (canalisation).
Fresh water tunnels from the rivers to be dammed for drinking, bathing and washing.
Gas and Steam turbine engines to supplement electricity.
Extensive rail networks for the country with the help of the Americans, Asians and the Europeans.

Nuclear Power lines for electricity and for Industries with the help of the Russians.

ALL THESE THINGS WILL BE INVISIBLE TO THOSE WHO HAVE NOT SEEN THIS BOOK.

I like to use this formula, only if the lords use me.

But if the lords refuse, I would operate with my formula in my business and I will still be happy.

The seven cats in control, must have attended any school in the country or abroad. Other people work with them and everyone is happy.

The seven platforms should be, I

Platform 1----B sr
Platform 2----B clinton
Platform 3----B jr
Platform 4----B Obama
Platform 5----B Jeb
Platform 6----Stephen,Mccain,Obasanjo and Jim
Platform 7----Putin, Aznar and Schroder

If we cannot find my six other people with me at any time, their positions remain vacant until we find them and anyone that behaves like a traitor goes to the third grade and stays there until he behaves well. Order is order and we must obey the rules.

In meetings
First grade----Best 7------ Red outfit
Second grade---Second best 7---- Blue outfit
Third grade----Group of Traitors or investigators.

Inner caucus
Outer caucus.

EVERYTHING IN ABSOLUTE SECRECY.

Motto- A BRY MUST RESCUE ANOTHER BRY, NO MATTER THE SITUATION.

If anyone, in the first grade is not available for a meeting, from the second grade, his type can represent him or her and there must be no discrimination.

CONCLUSION

To me, the lourdes or the lords, while they are cats themselves, control the cats, the negative, positive and the neutral ones. The lords know the other cats and the cats know them, they also know their voices and when they hear it, they act accordingly. The negative cats can be made by the lords or by the leaders to act and correct bad situations into good ones, if any situation is bad and seems uncontrollable, it means to me, that the lords or lourdes want it like that. And if the plan of salvation is to make a good situation to turn into a worse one and later back into a good situation in order to make a point, the lords can also allow that to happen, there is order in the universe and this is the reason why we should allow at all times, the good and powerful cats to rule. Under a normal circumstance, a cat must not kill another cat, simply because he likes to kill. A cat that is not smart will always lag behind while the smart ones are ahead of time, the new cats that are not yet well informed would always lag behind until they become smart probably through training. Therefore, to me, a peaceful situation occurs, if the leader wants it like that but if he also wants a reign of terror, it is also possible. Every leader writes his or her own record or history, for the people to read after. We should not blame any leader for controlling the way he likes and I think that we should cautiously follow them, and listen to every statement they are making at any time. Most actions of the leaders come from the decisions of the parliamentarians and the senators, and this is the reason why the cats in the two houses of assembly are always silent when dangerous things are happening. The leaders only make sure that the decisions backed up by the law, are in operation in the country.

I am always an advocate of world peace under a new world order, a new world in which sacred truths and happiness are upheld as very important, standard of living with freedom of individuals untrampled upon. The prototype of a new world order, as preached many years ago by President George Walker Bush, the forty-first (41) president of the United States of America.

There is an erroneous belief that the new world order is an order that makes possible, the changes of various old governments at a time. This is a false belief. Old and corrupt governments that are not contributing to the world economy can be changed and this must be done carefully without envy. It is very wrong to change a government, when the economy is in the top ten to top twenty in the world economy chart but another leader in the same government who knows what is happening, can assume power to continue to contribute to the progress of the same government, until the end of the time stipulated by the constitution of that land, and if power has to go to the other party, a cat in the other party who has been part of the government can take power and continue to make progress, possible. When this leader is confused or at the crossroads, not knowing how to continue, he can easily seek the help of his predecessor, who will be ready to help, for the sake of his nation. The new world order that I believe in, is the one in which all the existing nations come together as one to make new things possible and to make the upliftment of new standard of living to be possible. New technologies, learning and designs that creates awareness and lead to good type of living, also possible. Reduction of illiteracy, ignorance and poverty, if total removal is not possible, in most countries of the world. All the negative tendencies that will make the order, not to lead to world development and world peace, must be corrected. This is the new world order that everyone is talking about.

The example is already in Europe where the Europeans have common currency, common frontiers or borders, common transportation, common standard of living, poor European nations joining the European Union to lift up their economies.

I hope the Americans too will organise the American continents comprising the North and the South. As at now the North America, comprising of Canada and the United States Of America, is very standard and everyone wants to go there, to work, live and school, simply because the standard of living is excellent and everything is there but the South American continent comprising many nations like Chile, Argentina, Colombia, Peru, Brazil, etc., does not have anything and their economies cannot be compared with that of the North. All the South American people are running to North America and Europe to survive and why is this so? The new world order was advocated inside the American Parliament, many years ago but the Europeans were faster to start the implementation while the Americans still dont know what to do or that they know what to do but refused to act.

Maybe the Americans are using Europe as a test case and if this is so, it is normal. The principles of the new world order have survived in Europe and I give the credit to the great cats in this continent- the freemasons and the Illuminati.

I think the Americans, can start with common transportation, common currency-the dollar, common link and common borders like Europe, but the common American parliament uniting the North and the Southern people should be located in America and the language barrier solved with listening devices, just as the Europeans have done, the South Americans can use dollars in their continents like the Americans and with the common frontiers, the South Americans can enter America freely without visas, later the common currency issue can allow the South Americans to trade with the people of other continents in order to lift up their economies and to raise the standard of living. If the economies of the nations in the Southern continent are very good, most multi-national corporations would enter and invest, and this will put a stop to jumping of border fences into the American territory in the name of SURVIVAL by Mexicans and other South American people. The influx or inflow of desperate cats into North America will reduce and those that are already, inside will like to enjoy and return back home but if where they left is bad, they will never want to return, instead they will be looking for citizenship for permanent residence. The North Americans should treat their neighbors as human beings, by following the principle or the proclamation, they endorsed themselves, right inside their parliament, by allowing the South Americans to come in and go out of America without problems of visas, after all, they are whites like them and those that are in jails for breaking the immigration rules, if they are South Americans, should be released immediately. In the North America, there are many illegal immigrants who entered illegally because they want to survive and live good. One day, I was listening to a CNN program on immigrants and a woman was asked about her youthful dream and she said without fear, that her youthful dream or prayer, was to get into the North America at all COST, to study, work and live like the rest Americans. And she thanked God that the dream had been fulfilled, she studied, worked and had four children with the American man she met at school.

In Europe, an Austrian can come to Germany and a German can go to Austria without visas but the passports must be European, this is perfect. Even an African with the European resident permit can go to almost fifteen European nations freely without visas. The North Americans too, must make sure that the South Americans must show their valid passports when trying to enter the North America, but without visas, other cats from other continents can collect visas in order to enter both the North and the South America. The North America, as far as I am concerned, is the world's LAND OF PROMISE or ZION, everything is there, and I urge all of us to make this continent, a place where we would always fall back to, for answers or solutions, to world's problems.

On a final note, it is one thing to be a cat and it is another thing to be a good one. Up there, in the high societies, are lots of wealth and riches that are maintained by secrecy. A cat that cannot see or feel and keep quiet, constitutes danger or problems to those high societies and such a cat is easily removed or killed. There are also lots of rules guiding the high societies. The bible said in John 8 verse 32 that ye shall know the truth and the truth shall make you free. Yes, this is true, you see it, and you know it and you are happy. But I want to say that, sometimes too, someone can see and know the truth and if care is not taken by keeping silent, the truth that, that person has seen and known can kill him.

The less fortunate cats, who are not in the elite secret orders, call these high societies, crazy, because the actions of the cats in them, sometimes too, cannot be understood by the mass of the people. Only the qualified cats know the reasons why some actions are being taken.

Economically, the cats in the high societies, are rich and in good control. The social communities recognise their presence and things go on peacefully. Politically, they are known to control all the local and the national communities and everything therein.

Those people that work for the great cats can be said to be lesser cats who act as spies, and they are adequately rewarded.

In the high societies, each and every cat belongs to a school of thought, which is very secret, those that are of the same group, flocks together, do things in common and move ahead, in governments as leaders. Those that are of different group or school of thought but happen to be in government, are mostly watched and not trusted because they are just like the weeds among the real plants.

Up there, in the high societies, are lots of envy among the cats and a powerful cat sometimes can be tempted to oppress or dominate the others. In most cases, those cats that refused to be oppressed, always opt out of the government through resignation while those that accepts, remain.

Not all the leaders have this tendency to dominate and oppress, as some are very accommodating and caring. Most protests and riots, crop up, through some of the oppressed leaders, who find it easy to organise the unions and the mass of the people against the government. The mass of the people as I said earlier, are easy to be manipulated by these few ones through promises of jobs or through small incentives, which makes them radicalised to go to the street, to face armed policemen or soldiers.

To me, these few ones are the real problems and not the innocent mass of the people, who lose their lives fighting for a useless cause on the streets, in the name of fighting for rights.

This problem of a cat, trying to dominate the others, also often leads to civil war which is characterised by bombing and burning down of government and community properties. The problem escalates when the cats in the other nations of the world contribute to problems by assisting the rebels and the government of a nation, just in the name of liberation or freedom. I feel that these nations are trying to sell their military weapons, in order to rise up their economies but maybe I am wrong. The recent example is the civil war in Syria, where the Americans gave weapons to the rebels to fight against the government of Assad. President Vladmir Putin was against this step taken by the Americans and even the people of the world were surprised that the Americans can take such step. While the Americans want Assad to go, the Russians, want him to stay and reorganise Syria.

The questions, that crop up again, is, `why are these cats at loggerheads with each other and why have they chosen Syria as the battlefield?, Is it out of envy or is Syria having oil?, Is it political?, Why were the people, not ready to coexist peacefully?

The political analysts were all trying to find out the cause of the problem but to me, I think there is an ideological problem between the rightists and the leftists which can be resolved in a meeting. Different types of meetings were organised in different Arab nations and I think, the last one of such meetings is currently going on in Doha (June,2013). The American secretary of states, John Kerry, is always present in every meeting, and his pronouncement is that Assad used chemical weapons against his people and he must go. The meeting between the G8 member nations was also conducted to find a peaceful solution, to the problem of Syria. The whole world heard about the allegation that Assad used chemical weapon on his people but there was no evidence presented and while the Americans already armed the rebels against the government of Assad, the Russians and the rest of the world were busy condemning the act, this leads me to conclude that, not all the cats supported the American actions and that John Kerry should go back home to his job because the people already know the truth of the matter but if he has some bilateral relations meetings with the leaders of some countries, I think he can go ahead, travelling around.

Syria`s civil problem is ideological, and that the issue is -who controls Syria? Is it the rightists or the leftists? And if we look closely, we will see that Assad is always Pro-Russia and the Americans are not happy because they want him to be Pro-America, as they think that his group is in the minority. The thought that Assad group is in the minority in Syria, is false. The father was a president for many years in Syria-check the records. The cats can see that when the rebels were not retreating, another group called Hezbollah came in to help the government of Assad and this is to show everyone that he is not in the minority. There are still other groups, underground.

Most of the things, entering Syria are from Russia and other Arab nations and I don't see anything that is wrong with that, also before the civil war, there was peace and abundant life in Syria, until the leftists caused a problem there. The problem should be resolved because I think that the Russia of today is the same America of today. Putin is a Russian but he is always Pro-America and I know that America shares bilateral relations with Russia, therefore there is no problem.

Peaceful coexistence among the cats is the best option for world survival but it is common that in every community of good people, there are always JUDASES or traitors who would like to cause problems at all times. The problem of Syria is not a religious one and I think that, this is the reason why most of the people were against the action on Assad.

Cats that want top positions but cannot see the way to the top should go for various top management trainings, where they may receive intuitions and revelations, which would eventually lead them to the top. It is one thing to get to the top and it is another thing, to stay successfully in power. But we should not forget that, the constitution of every nation determines the limit by which every cat can stay in power. Let us all obey the laws and the orders, through our constitutions and by this act, we will all arrive at a strong and a peaceful world.

REFERENCES

a. HYPERLINK "http://www.wildlife-pictures-online.com/lion-information.html" \l "ixzz1O8ND6Z4x" _http://www.wildlife-

b. INCLUDEPICTURE "http://www.wildlife-pictures-online.com/image-files/lionpairinfo.jpg"* MERGEFORMATINET HYPERLINK "http://www.wildlife-pictures-online.com/lion_rctb-8622.html" INCLUDEPICTURE "http://www.wildlife-pictures-online.com/image- files/lion_rctb-8622s.jpg"\ MERGEFORMATINET_ HYPERLINK "http://www.wildlife-pictures-online.com/lion_rctb-8592.html" __ INCLUDEPICTURE "http://www.wildlife-picturesonline.com/imagefiles/lion_rctb-8592s.jpg" * MERGEFORMATINET ____

c. cia.gov --History and mission of CIA.

d. fbi.gov History/ intelligent operations

e. KGB - History and founded date

f. MOSSAD- History and founded date.

g. BND - History and founded date

i. British armed forces.co.uk

j. United States of America Military Strength Detail by the numbers Record Last Updated:7/1/2011 | Authored by Staff Writer

k. Germany Military Strength Detail by the numbers.
Authored by Staff Writer

l. Israel Military Strength Detail by the numbers.
Authored by Staff Writer

m.http://www.ancient-future.net/basics.html--Basic catholic beliefs

n. Mormons.org

i. http://www.businessinsider.com/canadas-f-35-decision-rafale typhoon-super-hornet-gripen2012-12?op=1#ixzz2EmMi7sIz

j. http://www.businessinsider.com/the-20-in-service-aircraft carriers-patrolling-the-world-today-2012

k. http://www.businessinsider.com/bi-x-47b-2012

l. The lost symbol by DAN BROWN

m.http://www.businessinsider.com/ why-the-drug-war-is-unwinnable-2013-2#ixzz2MVycg6c0

n. http://www.businessinsider.com/ how-chinese-hackers-steal-secrets-2013-2?op=1#ixzz2MWC8VZSv

o. http://www.answers.com/topic/ china-intelligence-and-security#ixzz2blZ5e8XK

p. ADVERSARY FOREIGN INTELLIGENCE OPERATIONS Section 3 Operations Security INTELLIGENCE THREAT HANDBOOK Interagency OPSEC Support Staff [April 1996 Revised May 1996]

q. CASTRO'S AMERICA DEPARTMENT Coordinating Cuba's Support for Marxist-Leninist Violence in the Americas by Rex A. Hudson The Cuban American National Foundation 1988

Other list of references

Compared and Contrasted, Tanks from World War I to the Present Day, by Martin J. Dougherty
Tanks of World Wars I and II, by George Forty
The Illustrated Encyclopaedia of the World's Tanks and Fighting Vehicles, by Christopher F. Foss
Jane's Tanks and Combat Vehicles Recognition Guide, by Christopher F. Foss
The Essential Vehicle Identification Guide, Post-war Armoured Fighting Vehicles 1945 - Present, by Michael E. Haskew

Bathurst, R. (1993) Intelligence and the Mirror: on creating an enemy, London:
Sage
Beasley, W.G. (1987) Japanese Imperialism, 1894-1945, Oxford: OUP
Benedict, R. (1946) The Chrysanthemum and the Sword: patterns in Japanese
culture, Cambridge, MA: Riverside
Booth, K. (1979) Strategy and Ethnocentrism, London: Croom Helm
Butow, R.J.C. (1961) Tojo and the Coming of War, Stanford: Stanford UP
Coox, A.D. (1985) Nomonhan: Japan against Russia, 1939, Stanford: Stanford
UP
Drea, E. (1998) In the Service of the Emperor: essays on the Imperial Japanesew
Army, Lincoln: Nebraska UP
Elphick, P. (1997) Far Eastern File: the intelligence war in the Far East, 1930-45,
London: Hodder & Stoughton
Gluck, C. (1985) Japan's Modern Myths: ideology in the late Meiji period, Princeton: Princeton UP
Gray, C. (1999) Modern Strategy, Oxford: OUP
Handel, M. (1989) War, Strategy and Intelligence, London: Frank Cass
Hayashi, S. (1959) Kogun: the Japanese Army in the Pacific War, Quantico: Marine Corps Association
Herman, M. (1996) Intelligence Power in Peace and War, Cambridge: CUP /
London: Royal Institute of International Affairs

Humphreys, L.A. (1995) The Way of the Heavenly Sword: The Japanese Army in the 1920s, Stanford: Stanford UP

Ike, N. (1967) Japan's Decision for War: records of the 1941 policy conferences, Stanford: Stanford UP

Jervis, R. (1976) Perception and Misperception in International Politics, Princeton: Princeton UP

Mercado, S. (2002) The Shadow Warriors of Nakano: a history of the Imperial Japanese Army's elite intelligence school, Washington, DC: Brassey's Morgan, F. (2003) Compellence and the Strategic Culture of Imperial Japan: implications for coercive diplomacy in the twenty-first century, Westport, CT: Praeger 17

Morley, J. (1994) The Final Confrontation: Japan's negotiations with the United States, 1941, selected translations from series taiheiyo senso e no michi: kaisen gaiko shi, English translation - Japan's Road to the Pacific War, NY: ColumbiaSwinson, A. (1968) Four Samurai: a quartet of Japanese army commanders in the Second World War, London: Hutchinson

Tsuji, M. (1993) Japan's Greatest Victory, Britain's Worst Defeat, NY: Sarpedon

Willmott, H.P. (1982) Empires in the Balance: Japanese and Allied Pacific strategies to April 1942, Annapolis: Naval Institute Press

Book Chapters:

Akagi, K. (2004) 'Leadership in Japan's Planning for War Against Britain', in B.

Bond and K. Tachikawa (eds), British and Japanese Military Leadership in the Far Eastern War, 1941-1945, Abingdon: Frank Cass, pp.53-63

Barnhart, M. (1984) 'Japanese Intelligence Before the Second World War: best case analysis', in E. May (ed.), Knowing One's Enemies: intelligence assessment before the two world wars, Princeton: Princeton UP, pp.424-55

Chapman, J.W.M. (1987) 'Japanese Intelligence, 1918-1945: a suitable case for treatment', in C. Andrew and J. Noakes (eds), Intelligence and International Relations, 1900-1945, Exeter: Exeter UP, pp.145-90 Coox, A.D. (1991) 'Japanese Intelligence in the Pacific Theater', W.T. Hitchcock (ed.), The Intelligence Revolution: a historical perspective, Washington, DC:

US
Air Force Academy, pp.197-202
Coox, A.D. (1992) 'Japanese Net Assessment in the Era Before Pearl Harbor', in

A.R. Millett and W. Murray (eds), Calculations, Net Assessment and the Coming of World War II, NY: Free Press, pp.258-98
Coox, A.D. (1988) 'The Effectiveness of the Japanese Military Establishment in the Second World War', in A.R. Millett and W. Murray (eds), Military Effectiveness, Volume III: The Second World War, Boston: Allen & Unwin, pp.1-44

Ikeda, K. (1982) 'Japanese Strategy in the Pacific War, 1941-1945', in I. Nish (ed.), Anglo-Japanese Alienation, 1919-52: papers of the Anglo-Japanese Conference on the history of the Second World War, Cambridge: CUP, pp.125-46
Assessment and the Conduct of the Pacific War, 1941-1945: the British-Indian and Imperial

Japanese armies in comparison', in War in History, Volume 14, No.1 (2007), pp.63-95.

(London, 1993); M. Handel, War, Strategy and Intelligence (London: Frank Cass, 1989), Chapter 5; M. Herman, Intelligence Power in Peace and War (Cambridge: CUP / London: Royal Institute of International Affairs, 1996);
cultural factors influence threat perception, see K. Booth, Strategy and Ethnocentrism (London: Croom Helm, 1979); R. Jervis, Perception and Misperception in International Politics (Princeton: Princeton UP, 1976).

W.G. Beasley, Japanese Imperialism, 1894-1945 (Oxford: OUP, 1987), Chapter 3; R.
Benedict, The Chrysanthemum and the Sword: patterns in Japanese culture (Cambridge, MA: Riverside, 1946), Chapter 4; C. Gluck, Japan's Modern Myths: ideology in the late Meiji period
(Princeton: Princeton UP, 1985), especially Chapters 1-2, and United States National Archives and Record Administration, College Park, MD (NARA 2), RG

165, M-1216, Roll 19, MID 2023-670, Revisions in Field Service Regulations, Translated document provided by US Military Attaché (Tokyo), 19 May 1925. The principle was articulated in the Japanese army's infantry manual as early as 1909. See Humphreys, 1995, p.15.

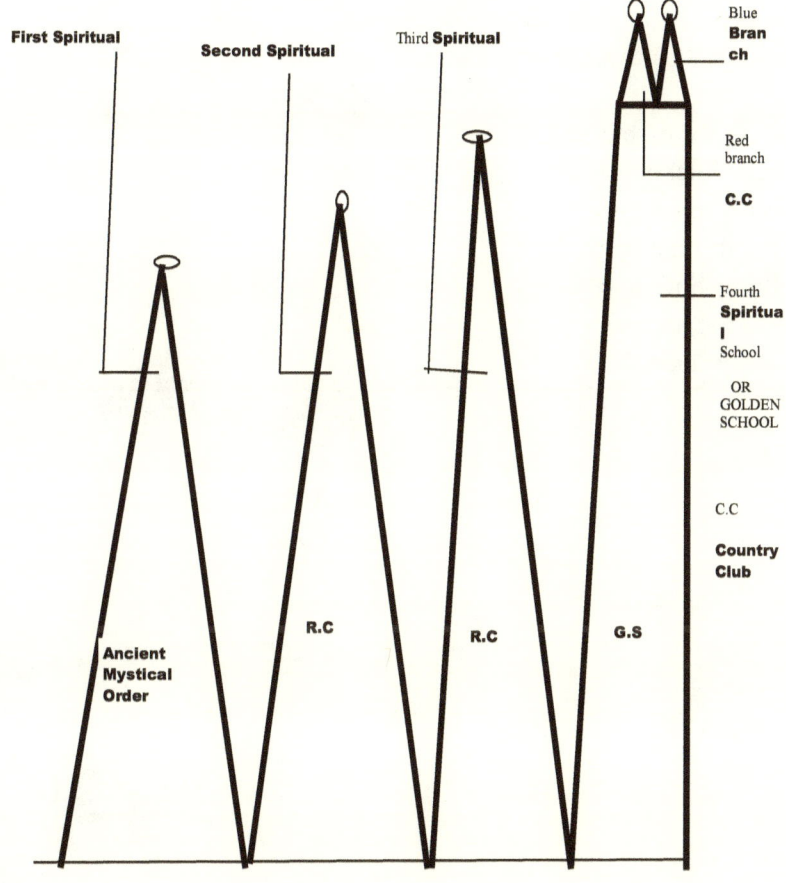

First Spiritual

Second Spiritual

Third **Spiritual**

Blue **Bran ch**

Red branch

C.C

Fourth **Spiritua l** School

OR GOLDEN SCHOOL

C.C

Country Club

Ancient Mystical Order

R.C

R.C

G.S

MY GOLDEN JOURNEY

79

Clues
LAUS DEO -Praise God

L -The stone square- Symbol of honesty and being true.
AU -Gold.
S -Sum total of all parts(S).
(Delta) -(D)-Symbol of change.
Mercury -(E)-Ancient alchemical symbol.
Ouroboros(O)-Symbol of wholeness.

41 Bush -Surname -B
42 Bill -First name-B
43 Bush -Surname -B
44 Barak-First name-B
45 Bush -Surname -B
46 ? -First name-?
47 ? -Surname -?

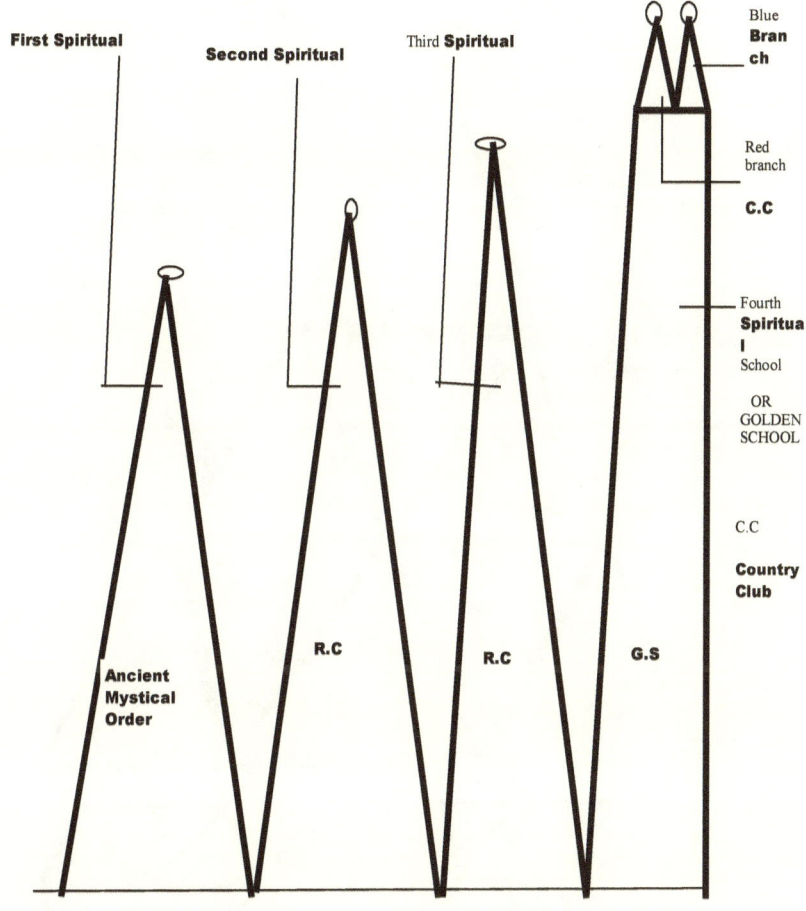

First Spiritual

Second Spiritual

Third **Spiritual**

Blue **Bran ch**

Red branch

C.C

Fourth **Spiritua l** School

OR GOLDEN SCHOOL

C.C

Country Club

Ancient Mystical Order

R.C

R.C

G.S

MY GOLDEN JOURNEY

PYTHAGORAS TRIANGLE
Pythagoras was the greatest cat that ever lived (One big triangle plus nine smaller ones = Ten)

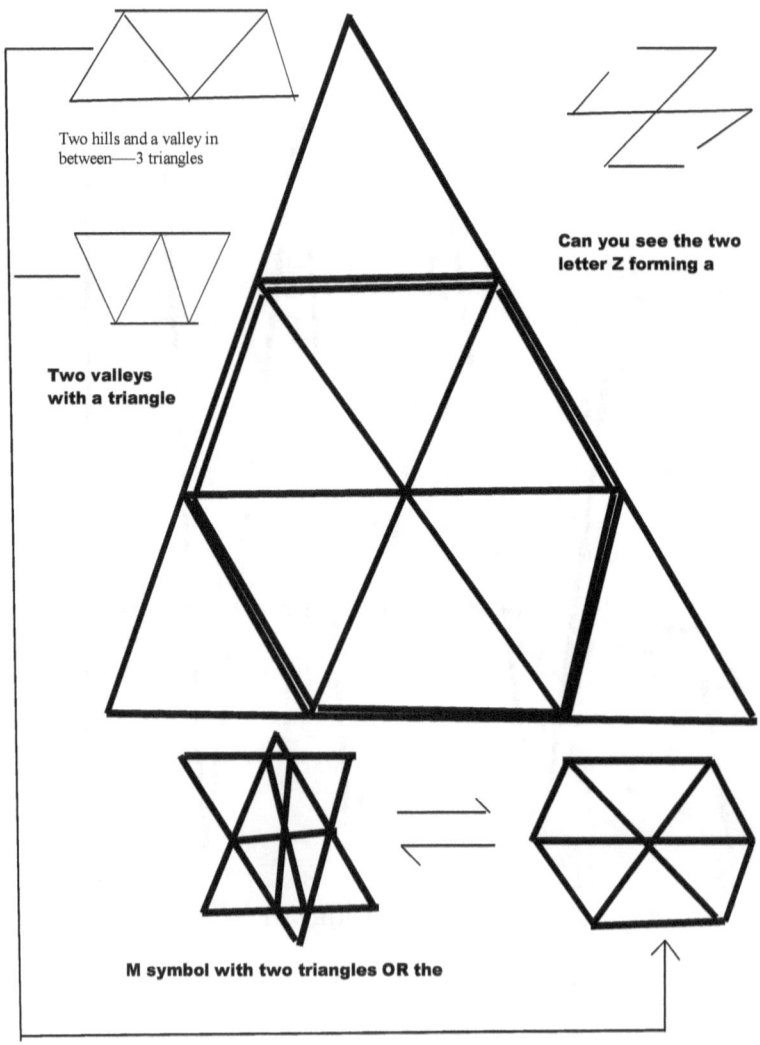

Two hills and a valley in between——3 triangles

Can you see the two letter Z forming a

Two valleys with a triangle

M symbol with two triangles OR the

Other cats that are qualified but were not chosen have been sidetracked by the great cats- the lords of the lords. But I know that the LORDS can show MERCY to any sidetracked cat, if it pleases them, through the pleadings of the other LORDS in the council of LORDS. No fighting or attack can resolve the problem, only pleadings and deliberations by the other LORDS in the council. Then the sequence can continue, further with B.

Franklin`s square(can have alphabets or numbers) and the alphabets below, if you look carefully formed interwoven waves like two triangles on each other- A GREAT M-SYMBOL

```
p F E E S E S N
R E T M P F H A
I R W E O O I G
M E E N N R M A
E N E T S H A S
D C N S I I A A
I E E R B R N K
F B L E L O D I
```

U-238
U-235
Difference = 3

Uranium with isotope 238
Uranium with isotope 235

Uranium is a nuclear material.

www.ingramcontent.com/pod-product-compliance
Lightning Source LLC
Chambersburg PA
CBHW032029290526
45786CB00011B/1187